THE LAPPS

THE LAPPS

ARTHUR SPENCER

Crane, Russak & Company Inc. New York
David & Charles   Newton Abbot   London   Vancouver

British Library Cataloguing in Publication Data

Spencer, Arthur
    This changing world, the Lapps.
    1. Lapps – Social life and customs
    I. Title
    947.1'7'03   DL971.L2

ISBN 0–7153–7531–8

© Arthur Spencer 1978

Printed in Great Britain
by Redwood Burn Limited Trowbridge
for David & Charles (Publishers) Limited
Brunel House Newton Abbot Devon

Published in the United States of America
by Crane, Russak & Company, Inc.
347 Madison Avenue New York New York 10017

ISBN 0–8448–1263–3
Library of Congress Catalog Card Number 77–88165

Published in Canada
by Douglas David & Charles Limited
1875 Welch Street North Vancouver BC

CONTENTS

ACKNOWLEDGEMENTS

Of the many people who have so generously contributed their time and knowledge to the preparation of this book I should like to record my special indebtedness to Dr E.-J. Lindgren Utsi and Mikel Utsi, of Cambridge and Aviemore, whose great knowledge, wide experience and splendid library were unstintingly placed at my disposal. My thanks are due also to Professor Ørnulv Vorren, of Tromsø, and Professor Kallio and the staff of the Sub-Arctic Research Institute at Kevo. I am grateful, too, to the Finnish, Norwegian and Swedish authorities for their valuable help in many ways. Finally, I must pay tribute to my wife's encouragement and practical support, whether when camping in the snow or in typing my manuscript.

FOREWORD

The land of the Lapps is a magical world. The senses are entranced, the imagination stirred, by its sparkling snows, its reindeer, its sledges and its lively, colourful, people. In summer the sun shines the day through on majestic vistas of mountains and fjords, long valleys gay with flowers, dark forests and glittering lakes. Yet such an accepted and idyllic picture masks harsher realities. The climate is severe, the terrain difficult, the winters long, cold and perpetually dark. The Lapps, a small, remote people, scattered over a vast area of northernmost Europe, have been the pawns of powerful neighbours since the days of the Vikings. Skilful hunters who clothed the nobles of medieval Europe in furs, famous sorcerers of old, consummate craftsmen who developed a unique reindeer culture, they are now under attack from forces greater and more insidious than free-booting traders or punitive missionaries.

Many though the material benefits of recent decades have been, they have tended nevertheless to harm the Lapps' traditional culture and to threaten their national identity. The minerals and timber of Lapland go to feed the insatiable appetites of alien industries. Ancient grazing-grounds, lakes and rivers rich in fish, are ruined by hydro-electric development. The claims of a minority are brushed aside for the 'common good' of the larger state. And over all loom the implications of Lapland's new status as one of the key strategic areas in the world. No wonder that the Lapps, with their long survival as a people at stake, have become more politically minded and organised to resist 'technocratic colonialism'.

From Roman historians to the newspaper articles, travel books and learned journals of today the Lapps have intrigued the world. Not all that is written about them is worthy of the theme; of late, they have too often been treated somewhat condescendingly as little more than photographic subjects, often only one small group or a particular district being considered. Concurrently, the greater specialisation of Lapp studies has produced a mass of valuable material which, however, is necessarily limited by the authors' disciplines, is not readily accessible to the general reader, and is not usually in English. This book, therefore, tries to give a broad, accurate survey of all the Lapps, to do justice to a steadfast and attractive people, and to arouse the reader's interest sufficiently to pursue the subject further. Many important matters are inevitably treated too cursorily or too categorically, but I hope the balance will be considered fair. Historical and traditional aspects have been stressed because, in an era of widespread decolonisation, they, and not the emergence of yet another minority's national aspirations, are the essential stuff of Lapp life in the eyes of the world.

Lapp words are, for convenience, generally given in the text in the central (or northern) Lappish form; this dialect is understood by three-quarters of all Lapps and is the official written Lappish in Norway and Sweden. In the text I have given, when necessary, the English translation of the titles of works I refer to, even when no English version is available, as will be evident from the Bibliography.

A.S.

I
THE LAND AND ITS PEOPLE

The environment

The Lapps today live in the far north of Europe, mainly above the Arctic Circle. Their land is a crescent of wild country stretching from the rugged coast of Norway across the north of Norway, Sweden, Finland and the Soviet Union as far east as the Kola Peninsula on the White Sea. They have occasional settlements in suitable terrain in the mountainous backbone of Scandinavia as far south as Lake Femund in central Norway and northern Dalecarlia in Sweden. Formerly, especially in Finland, they lived further south. Their traditional way of life flourished until recently but has now almost disappeared. It is dominated by the seasonal extremes of climate and the bold topography of the vast and varied region of some 200,000 square miles which they inhabit. It provides an outstanding example of man's adaptation to his environment; and for centuries has been a source of wonder and lively interest for other peoples living in very different and easier circumstances.

In most of Lapland in winter the sun is never seen for weeks, in fact for up to seventy days at 72°N. In summer, for from eighteen days on the Arctic Circle (66°32′N) to eighty-eight at 72°N, it never sets, providing the well publicised spectacle of 'the midnight sun'. Most of the region is covered with snow for up to two-thirds of the year, the higher mountains permanently. On the coast the Gulf Stream exercises a moderating influence: the mean annual extreme temperatures at Vardø, for example, range from 18°C to−17°C (65° to 2°F). Winters are warmer than in

9

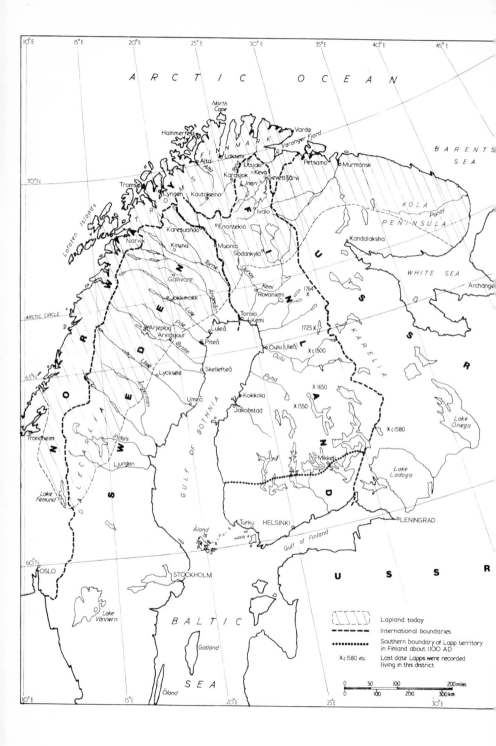

ARCTIC OCEAN

BARENTS SEA

North Cape

Hammerfest
Vardø
Varanger Fjord
Alta
Lakselv
Utsjoki
Kevo
Petsamo
Murmansk
Karasjok
Inari
Sevettijärvi
Tromsø
Lyngen
Kautokeino
Ivalo
KOLA PENINSULA
Ponoy
70°N
Enontekiö
Karesuando
Kandalaksha
Kiruna
Muonio
Sodankylä
WHITE SEA
Gällivare
Ounas
Torne
Kemi
Rovaniemi
1764 X
Archangel
Jokkmokk
Lule
Kemi
Arjeplog
Pite
Tornio
1725 X
Arvidsjaur
Byske
Luleå
KARELIA
ARCTIC CIRCLE
Piteå
Oulu (Uleå)
X c 1500
Lycksele
Skellefteå
Oulu
Ume
65°N
Umeå
Pyhä
Kokkola
X 1650
Jakobstad
X 1550
X c 1580
Ångerman
Trondheim
Indals
X c 1580
Lake Onega
Ljungan
Mikkeli
Lake Ladoga
Lake Femund
Turku HELSINKI
LENINGRAD
Åland Is
60°N
Gulf of Finland
OSLO
STOCKHOLM
U S S R
Lake Vännern
BALTIC
Gotland
SEA
Öland

NORWAY SWEDEN FINLAND RUSSIA KARELIA DALECARLIA LAPLAND LOFOTEN ISLANDS GULF OF BOTHNIA

Lofoten Islands
Narvik

////		Lapland today
– – –		International boundaries
••••••		Southern boundary of Lapp territory in Finland about 1100 AD
X c 1580 etc		Last date Lapps were recorded living in this district

0 50 100 200 miles
0 100 200 300 km

Oslo and the sea is free of ice. Inland, however, it is both much colder and much hotter: at Karasjok on the central plateau – Finnmarksvidda – mean annual extremes are 27°C to −42°C (81° to −44°F), and −51°C (−60°F) has been recorded. The short, intense summers are surprisingly hot. Indeed, in summer, Lapland often vies with the Mediterranean as the hottest part of Europe. Moreover, ultra-violet radiation is unusually strong – and for all the twenty-four hours of the day. In winter, by contrast, the long darkness is often lightened by the colourful, eerie shimmer of the Northern Lights.

Precipitation in the region is less than might be expected. It varies from about 40in (102cm) a year on the west coast to 12in (30cm) or so in the east, and occurs mainly as snow from November to April. There is considerable cloud much of the year and the high plateau in particular is windy, with violent blizzards in winter. Temperatures change suddenly and drastically: this is a serious matter to reindeer herders when a quick thaw, followed by a sharp frost, produces a layer of ice close to the ground too thick for the animals to dig through to reach their winter feed – the notorious *flen*.

In other ways too, the natural balance is delicately poised so that a slight shift may bring sometimes spectacular changes. The periodic swarming of the lemming (*Lemmus lemmus*) provides the best-known illustration of this and has long aroused the curious and credulous interest of the world. So suddenly do millions of these small rodents appear in a favourable year that it was long believed – and well into the nineteenth century – that they were generated by special clouds and fell from the sky. The suicidal manner in which they press on, sometimes swimming out to sea until they drown, has also captured the world's imagination. The periodic ravages of the caterpillar of a geometer moth (*Oporinia autumnata*) or the failure in successive years for no detectable cause of the cloudberry (*Rubus chamaemorus*) to set its valuable fruit are other, less known, but economically more important, examples of such critical shifts in the natural balance. When these caterpillars swarm they destroy their host plant, the upland birch-tree, a major source of fuel and

1 Lapland now and in the past

fodder, so that part of North Finland ten years after the latest infestation in 1966 looked as if a forest fire had swept through them.

This belt of dead and blackened trees also illustrates two other important aspects of the region's ecology. One is the prevalence of often sharply defined micro-climates reflecting the marked changes in altitude and orientation in mountainous country: the lower limit of the *Oporinia* damage runs across the flanks of mountains in a line as straight as if it has been deliberately drawn. The snow-line and the tree-line provide similar, but more widespread, illustrations of abrupt changes. The second aspect is the slow regeneration of damaged life in such harsh conditions. This, it is worth noting, applies to the soil itself, geologically young, thin, frozen most of the year, and lacking humus. In recent years wheeled or tracked vehicles (and in places the feet of tourists) have done considerable damage, not to mention the effects of this increased activity on the old culture of the Lapps themselves.

To survive in such an environment plants, animals and men have developed many subtle and distinctive adaptations. These inevitably have been determined both by the climatic factors described above and the different characteristics of Lapland's four main geographical regions. These may conveniently be described as: the Arctic coast of Norway and the north-western part of the Soviet Union with deeply indented fjords and big river valleys; the mountain chain between Norway and Sweden – Kjölen, 'the Keel', as it is called – with perpetual snow at height and important valleys running from NW to SE on its long eastern flank; the rolling central plateau east and south of the mountains; the low-lying forest areas of north Sweden, north Finland and the southern parts of the Kola Peninsula with thousands of lakes in the eastern part where it merges into the Siberian taiga.

The three divisions of traditional Lapp culture broadly conform with these regional distinctions. They are: the Sea, or Coast, Lapps, the largest group – fisherman and crofters long settled on the shores of the Arctic Ocean and the banks of the great rivers feeding it; the Mountain Lapps, the real Lapps to most people, nomads accompanying their reindeer in their seasonal migrations, with sledges and portable tents and belongings; and the semi-nomadic Forest Lapps in permanent homes with some cultivated land, migrating only short distances with their reindeer. The Skolt Lapps, in north Finland and the Kola Peninsula west of Murmansk and Kandalaksha, combine fishing, hunting and reindeer-breeding in the ancient tradition. The Kola Lapps in north-western Russia have now been collectivised and raise large herds of reindeer by more modern methods of stock-breeding. Some authorities have a separate classification of Fisher Lapps for the Skolt and those Forest Lapps settled by lakes and rivers, whose main occupation is fishing.

Animals and plants

The reindeer (*Rangifer tarandus*) is the typical and the most important animal in Lapland. Its dominant influence on Lapp life for centuries is discussed at length in Chapter 3. Meanwhile it should be noted how, like other permanent residents of the region, it is beautifully adapted to face its harsh surroundings. Its coat has hollow hairs and is one of the best insulators known. Its camel-like feet enable it to traverse the snow with ease. Its white rump, the unique structure of its toe-tendons which click as the foot moves, and the scent-glands in its hooves, serve to keep the herds together in mountain murk and the long, dark winters.

On the coast seals, mainly harp (*Phoca groenlandica*) and ringed (*Phoca hispida*), were a comparable major source of food (also of oil and clothing) right up to the closing years of the nineteenth century, and some are still caught. Whales too, were hunted. These sea mammals are protected from the cold by a layer of fat beneath their skins. Several of Lapland's land mammals have developed the same defence – lemmings, for example. Lemmings and other small creatures also keep warm in winter by making burrows in the snow. Other animals, bears and foxes for instance, have for the same reason acquired larger bodies and smaller extremities than members of their species in warmer lands, the former conserving, the latter reducing, the loss of their body-heat. The coat of the Arctic or blue fox (*Canis lagopus*) and Arctic hare (*Lepus timidus*), turn white in winter with the same effect, as does that of the stoat (*Mustela erminea*) with its valuable ermine winter skin. The cells with dark pigment are emptied at this change, becoming minute air pockets which act as insulators. The white colour also has a survival value as camouflage against the snow. Less obviously, in spring and autumn when the sun is strong, it reflects heat and prevents the animals from getting too hot. Birds such as the ptarmigan (*Lagopus mutus*) or the snow bunting (*Plectophrenax nivalis*) to go through the same process. They, and the animals, also grow a fluffy inner layer to their coat in winter. Bears and squirrels (*Sciurus vulgaris*) avoid the full rigour of winter by hibernating. The beaver (*Castor fiber*) lives in water above freezing-point.

Of the many birds which make Lapland an ornithologist's paradise most are summer migrants. Permanent residents include various grouse, capercaillies, predators such as the eagle owl (*Bubo bubo*) and several hawks. There is a lot of local migration to the coast or northern Europe. Game birds, particularly the willow-grouse (*Lagopus lagopus*) and ptarmigan, are an important source of food. Various ducks and sea birds such as puffins (*Fratercula arctica*) are eaten as well. Ducks are still sometimes provided with nesting boxes so that their eggs may be collected, while the down of the eider duck (*Somateria mollissima*) was formerly an important commodity. Larger predators, especially the golden eagle (*Aquila chrysaëtos*) and scavengers like the raven (*Corvus corax*) are a menace to young, or injured, reindeer. Lapland's biggest bird is the whooper swan (*Cygnus cygnus*), some 60in long; the bluethroat (*Cyanosylvia suecica*) is the most tuneful. Many birds well-known further south are also found – the ubiquitous house sparrow (*Passer domesticus*), meadow pipit (*Anthus pratensis*), and several thrushes; upland birds such as brambling (*Fringilla mondifringilla*), wheatear (*Oenanthe oenanthe*) and dipper (*Cinclus cinclus*); and waterfowl – shags (*Phalacrocorax aristotelis*), cormorants (*Phalacrocorax carbo*), teals (*Anas crecca*), mallard (*Anas platyrhynchos*) and many gulls. Characteristic water-birds are the black-throated diver or Pacific loon (*Colymbus arcticus*), red-throated diver or red-throated loon (*Colymbus stellatus*), red-breasted merganser (*Mergus serrator*) and goosander (*Mergus merganser*). The many rarities include the bar-tailed godwit (*Limosa lapponica*), the great grey owl (*Stryx nebulosa*), rough-legged buzzard (*Buteo lagopus*), gyr falcon (*Falco rusticolus*), golden plover (*Charadrius apricarius*), lapland bunting (*Calcarius lapponicus*) and Siberian tit (*Parus cinctus*).

There are comparatively few species of animals in Lapland. The biggest is the bear, which has long held a place of honour and, in the old religions of the North, had an almost sacred status (p 98ff). Its numbers are at present increasing. Wolves (*Canis lupus*) are now scarce, though their depredations made the headlines only a couple of decades ago: they are commonest in north Finland. The vicious wolverine or glutton (*Gulo gulo*), a large weasel as big as a badger, is still fairly widespread. Several species of foxes are common. Lynxes (*Lynx lynx*) are found in southerly forests, the elk or moose (*Alces alces*) is expanding its range northwards. There are badgers (*Meles meles*) and otters (*Lutra lutra*) in lower-lying districts, and various small rodents everywhere. The classic fur-bearing animals – sable (*Martes zibellina*) and marten (*Martes martes*) – are now sadly reduced in numbers. Domestic cattle can be raised along the whole coast and in the lower inland districts.

Fish abound, both in salt and fresh water. The fjords and rivers of Lapland have some of the finest fishing for salmon (*Salmo salar*) in the world. Offshore there are vast shoals of various types of cod (*Gadidae spp.*). Alpine char (*Salvelinus alpinus*) and salmon trout (*Salmo trutta*) flourish in mountain lakes. In lakes and rivers lower down, whitefish (*Coregonus spp.*), a close relation of the vendace, grayling (*Thymallus thymallus*), bleak (*Alburnus alburnus*), burbot (*Lota lota*), trout (*Salmo trutta fario*), perch (*Perca fluviatilis*) and pike (*Esox lucius*) are a major source of the Lapps' food. There are many edible shellfish on the coast, and fresh-water mussels (*Margaritana margaritifera*) are taken for pearls.

These fish, and many of the birds, feed on the vast swarms of insects which, from about ten days after the thaw until the first frost, are a major feature of the Lapland summer. Mosquitoes and blackflies (mainly species of *Aëdes* and *Theobaldia*) are as big a nuisance as anything in the tropics. They are however not malarial and irritate, rather than incapacitate, by their myriad bites. Nor do they fly, if there is a wind or unless the temperature is over 10°C (50°F). Of the larger flies, two – the nose-botfly (*Cephenomyia trompe*) and the warble-fly (*Oedomagaena tarandi*) – are a serious scourge of the reindeer. Several tabanid flies – horseflies, the 'clegs' of the Scottish Highlands – are a painful nuisance to man.

Plant life is varied and locally luxuriant, ranging from the upper limits of vegetation on the edge of the snow, through tundra-like fells and lush bogs to reedy forest lakes and grassy meadows bright with flowers. True tundra is ground frozen from about 3 to 250ft (1–75m), which is not the case in Lapland, though areas of true tundra are found. There is a clear demarcation at the tree-line which, botanically, is the boundary between the Arctic and the sub-Arctic zones. Highest up grows snow-patch vegetation, various species of the long-lived, hardy, lichens; specialised, ground-hugging plants, tough and long-rooted, such as *Diapensia lapponica* and rushes (*Juncus alpinus, J. trifidus*). Next, stunted specimens of plants abundant below the tree-line, appear – larger lichens (particularly the reindeer's chief winter food, *Cladonia rangiferina* and *Cladonia alpestris*); sphagnum mosses, bog rosemary (*Andromeda polyfolia*), various heathers (*Calluna* and *Erica spp.*) and berried plants. The first trees are dwarf birches (*Betula nana, B. tortuosa*) and low willows (*Salix spp.*) the protective value of which is rapidly apparent in the stronger growth of the floor cover – heathers, reindeer-lichens, bearberry (*Arctostaphylos ursa-uvi*), crowberry (*Empetrum nigrum*) and bilberries (*Vaccinium myrtillus*). At lower levels there are vast belts of coniferous forest, mainly pines (*Pinus spp.*) with spruce (*Picea spp.*) predominating further east, with lusher undergrowth and grassy clearings. In damper places, willows and alders (*Alnus glutinosa*) predominate. The juniper (*Juniperus communis*) is common on open ground, the aspen (*Populus alba*) in milder areas, where apples and fruit bushes, such as blackcurrants, will also grow.

Of the many interesting plants, which are fully dealt with in specialist publications, only those that are of value to the Lapps, common enough to be typical, or of rarity value, deserve a mention here. Angelica (*Angelica archangelica*) is eaten with relish by man and beast alike. It is a valuable anti-scorbutic, as are the berries mentioned earlier. The leaves of the mountain sorrel (*Oxyria digyna*) or of the sheep's sorrel (*Rumex acetosa*) are mixed with curdled reindeer milk, which the Lapps then freeze for winter use (*juobmo*). The root of the blue sow-thistle (*Cicerbita macrophylla*) is also eaten. Various fungi (mainly *Boletus spp.*) are included in the diet of both Lapp and reindeer. Beard lichens (*Alectoria spp.*) from tree branches in winter and navel lichen (*Gyrophora spp.*) in spring, supplement the reindeer's seasonal diet which, in summer, includes horsetails (*Equisetum spp.*) and bogbean (*Menyanthes trifoliata*) as well as most green shoots and a variety of grasses. The main cultivated crops are rye, barley, potatoes and turnips.

The great profusion of some of the commoner plants in suitable habitats is a memorable feature of Lapland. Some of those mentioned – especially the lichens, grey-green or tawny, and the purple heather – contribute to the scenic effect. Globe-flowers (*Trollius europaeus*) and kingcups (*Caltha palustris*) grow in great yellow sheets, with cotton grass (*Eriophorum angustifolium*) in drifts of white like rippling snow. The ground is starred with lovely little plants – butterworts (*Pinguicula spp.*) and sundews (*Drosera spp.*) in damp places, the 'Lapland rose' (*Rhododendron lapponicum*), the shy twin-flower (*Linnaea borealis*), the mountain avens (*Dryas octopetala*), dwarf cornel (*Cornus suecica*), mountain pansy (*Viola lutea*) and many others. There are rarer flowers too, the Alpine gentian (*Gentiana nivalis*), Alpine milk-vetch (*Astragalus alpinus*), blue heath or 'Lapp heather' (*Phyllodoce caerulea*) and the coralroot orchid (*Corallorhiza trifida*), as well as numerous other plants which attract the botanist.

Early inhabitants

The earliest known remains of human habitation in Fennoscandia, the Komsa culture of about 8,000 years ago, are on the coast of Lapland. From that day to this, sites on Varanger Fjord have been occupied continuously. At the beginning of the Christian era, a culture recognisable as Lapp, with skeletons identified as Lapp and with iron and bone artefacts, replaced that of the Stone Age there. The first written reference to them, by the Roman historian Tacitus, also dates from this period. Thus it is reasonable to conclude that the Lapps were in their present territories 2,000 or so years ago. The Komsa finds, however, opened up the possibility that they, or at least their ancestors, had been there thousands of years earlier; and it is on this question that modern discussions on the Lapps' origins and arrival in Lapland have turned.

There has long been among the Lapps an old tradition that they have always lived in the north. The first Lapp to write about his people in their mother tongue, Johan Turi, in his *Book of Lapland* (1910) thus records it: 'From the very earliest times they have been here in Lapland; and when, in the beginning, the Lapps lived by the sea-coast, there was not a single other person.'

The authority of the early foreign savants who discussed the matter tended, however, to obscure the Lapps' own views. Scheffer, in his epoch-making study, *Lapponia* (1673), claims that they came from the 'Scythian Orient' at a time of widespread migration in the first millenium BC, and were related to the Finns and the Samoyeds. To Linnaeus (1755) they were 'Asiatics'. The 'Father of Anthropology', J. F. Blumenbach, classed them as 'Mongols', an erroneous view to which his eminence gave currency until quite recently, long after a more scientific approach had established that they were of Caucasoid, not Mongoloid, stock. The important role played by philologists in early discussions of the subject undoubtedly sustained the eastern view, since Lappish is related to the eastern Ural-Altaic languages. Nevertheless, even before the Komsa finds, the accepted account was being questioned.

From the middle of the nineteenth century the growth of new disciplines and the improvement of scientific method produced new evidence to show that the matter was much more complex than previously thought. Physiologists discovered in the Lapps certain unique characteristics which could be explained only by the hypothesis that the Lapps were, or at any rate were descended from, an original Arctic people. Geologists and botanists proved that large areas of Lapland, including a coastal strip, had been free of ice during the latest Ice Age. The traditionalists counter-attacked with a great wealth of traditional evidence. But their case has been steadily weakened by archaeological and other new discoveries. It should, incidentally, be stated that it has not yet been proved that the Komsa people were of Lapp type.

The present view, to which Finnish, Norwegian and Swedish experts have all contributed, is a reasonable synthesis of earlier, somewhat too exclusive, theories. It is that, at the end of the Pleistocene Ice Age, the ancestors of the Lapps, a hunting people adapted to cold conditions, followed the receding ice northwards from somewhere in western Asia. They spread into Finland and the lower-lying parts of modern Lapland, possibly helped by a frozen Baltic Sea, and then, about 8,000 years ago, along the ice-free northern coast. As conditions improved – there was a very warm period about 4000 BC – they moved further inland. Others followed at different times, urged on by population pressures further east, of which there is good evidence from the Balkans and western Asia. The Finns for instance moved into their land from the south-east around 1000 BC in response to such a situation and in turn began to push the Lapps northward. Thus, when they first came to the world's notice, the Lapps were inhabiting most of Finland and Karelia, as well as their present territories. Parts of Norway and Sweden further south were already occupied by the ancestors of the present inhabitants from about 5000 BC.

The Lapps

An account of a people's racial characteristics and behaviour is always fraught with difficulties, but an attempt must be made to give one. For the Lapps, problems of nomenclature and identification complicate the issue. To others the Lapps have been known by various names, but to themselves (see note on dialect in Foreword) they are 'Sameh' (singular 'Same') and their country is 'Sameätnam' (land of the 'Sameh'). Since World War II Norwegians and Swedes have officially referred to them as 'Samer' – a meaningless English version, 'Sames' being adopted by some scholars. The Finns too have recently begun to follow suit. Somewhat confusingly, the usual Norwegian word for Lapp is 'Finn'; hence northern Norway is called Finnmark (the Lapp border region). It is under this description, latinised as 'Fenni', that the Lapps first appear in written records. The first use of the word Lapp as a placename, 'Lappia', dates from the thirteenth century. It is thought to be derived from an archaic Finnish word with some connotation such as 'outcast'. The name gained currency, in its appropriate forms, in Swedish, Finnish and Russian, and remains in popular use in these countries, as it does outside Scandinavia.

There is, however, no accepted definition of a Lapp. Kinship and descent are obvious criteria. The proud, reindeer-owning, Mountain Lapps maintain that a Lapp is a person who owns reindeer, although for centuries there have been undoubted Lapps who do not. National censuses have not enumerated Lapps as a separate group for many years, and then only on the basis of those who chose to declare that they spoke Lappish. In view of the bad treatment of Lapps for generations, many of them refrained from doing so. Hence such statistics are misleadingly low as well as out of date. Recently more enlightened policies towards minority groups and the growth of a Lapp national consciousness have encouraged more of them to acknowledge their inheritance, but their exact number remains a matter of conjecture. Most authorities put the figure at about 35,000, of whom 20–22 thousand live in Norway, 8–10 thousand in Sweden, 3–4 thousand in Finland and about 2–3 thousand in the Soviet Union. A recent Swedish estimate, however, gives 40,000, which is in line with the trend noted above, that more Lapps admit to being such.

Despite local variations and very many obvious exceptions there is a distinct Lapp racial type: the picture of the 'typical Lapp' which, however unscientific, comes to mind. This person is short – just over 5ft (1·5m) for men, about 4in (10cm) less for women, though, as with other peoples, the average height is increasing in modern conditions. There are also many more blond, blue-eyed Lapps than formerly. The legs are short but, contrary to popular accounts and droll sketches, not bowed: it is the traditional costume which gives this effect. The hair is straight and dark, the face pear-shaped with sparse beard, the skin olive, the features small and neat with a straight nose and high cheek-bones. Eyes are predominantly brown or grey and, except for a few eastern Lapps, are not slant, as they lack the epicanthic fold of the Mongoloid people. Until old age, eyesight is remarkably keen. The Lapps are unusually short-headed (average cephalic index 84). Type A blood groups, particularly the primarily European A2, predominate. In peoples east of the White Sea it is abruptly replaced by Type B. Anastomoses in the blood system are especially well adapted to cold. Lapps are strong and nimble, with a characteristic springy gait and have great stamina. The

Norwegian explorer, Amundsen, sent two Lapps to investigate the interior of Greenland in 1883. Their claim to have travelled 290 miles on skis in 57 hours being doubted on their return home, one of them took part in a race in north Sweden, which he won, covering 137 miles in just over 21 hours. The above qualities were put to good use in World War II when parties of Lapps, in particular Mikel Utsi, who now has a herd of reindeer in Scotland, and his late brother Paulus, a major Lapp poet, rescued many Norwegian refugees in the northern mountains.

Descriptions of the Lapps' behaviour and personal qualities have been distorted by cultural conflicts. When priests introduced Christianity they gave the Lapps a bad name as heathens. When the crops that Swedish settlers had planted on the Lapps' traditional grazing ground were eaten by reindeer returning from the mountains, they were dubbed thieving rogues. A more balanced view is that, like all peoples, they have good qualities and bad, and several which set them apart from their southern neighbours. For example, the northern Lapps are merrier, more sociable and more hospitable than Swedes and Norwegians. The southern Lapps, however, tend to be melancholic and introspective, but more loquacious than the northerners. Lapps as a people are very independent and resourceful, as they have to be, and extremely observant. Ties of family and a feeling of solidarity with other Lapps are highly developed. They are artistic, deft craftsmen, with a strong appreciation of materials, design and colour. They have always been known for their peaceful ways and so traditionally (and also because they have so often been the weaker party) tend to rely on guile to outwit, rather than on force to overcome, their adversaries. Commercially, this trait gained them an undeserved reputation for cheating, as did the convivial atmosphere of trade-fairs for drunkenness. Similarly, they are initially wary, even suspicious, of strangers. On the other hand, on their own ground and in harsh conditions, they are self-assured and effective, and many a less adequate Scandinavian neighbour had benefited from their generous help with food or shelter. Like other nomads, though orderly and systematic in their tents, they tend to be untidy in permanent homes. The seasonal nature of their life compels them to work erratically, so that they sometimes appear lazy. Possibly as a legacy of their old ecstatic religion they are often considered excitable, especially in groups and indoors. They have a well-developed sense of personal property which, allied to their self-reliance and versatility, ensures that a self-respecting family can, and is expected to, fend for itself. Therefore, anyone who asks for help in everyday matters is considered feckless, with consequent damage to his reputation.

2

THE LAPPS IN HISTORY

General considerations

Whether the Lapps were the first inhabitants of their land remains an open question. References in classical literature, however, provide evidence for their being there about 2,000 years ago. Later authors offer a consistent, though sporadic, account of their ancient life up to the Middle Ages. With the sixteenth century the first systematic studies appear, reflecting both the growth of knowledge and the national interests of northern states. Thereafter up to the present there is a steady increase in historical studies of the Lapps. The story is a complex and sometimes sad one of a small people's relations with their powerful neighbours. In discussing it several general considerations should be borne in mind.

The first is that throughout history there have been two main, but not mutually exclusive, areas of contact between the Lapps and other peoples. One is the Arctic coast, with its ready access by sea and fairly easy approach through the valleys of north Finland. The other is the forest and lake country of north Sweden and Finland, including the headlands of the Gulf of Bothnia, a region with few obstacles to entry from further south. Each has made its separate contribution to Lapp history. A second consideration is the changing circumstances of the states which have determined Lapland's fate. With a sovereign, central, government for centuries, prosperous, progressive and more populous than other Scandinavian countries, Sweden has played the major role.

She ruled Finland from the Viking Age to the Napoleonic Wars. From 1814 to 1905 she was the senior partner in a union with Norway, which from the Middle Ages to that date had been little more than a backwater of the Danish kingdom. Finland gained independence as recently as 1917, having been a Russian grand duchy since the break with Sweden in 1809. Russia herself became a unitary state only in the eighteenth century. Before then the eastern Lapps had to deal with the small, but predatory, independent kingdoms of Karelia and Novgorod. Since the Bolshevik revolution the Soviet Union, in her treatment of the Lapps, as in other matters, has gone her separate way. The changes involved in all this, in national frontiers, tax liability, land tenure, even education were, until very recently, too often detrimental to the Lapps and have had profound economic and psychological ill-effects.

Finally it is worth noting that the history of the Lapps has been almost entirely written by other people. They themselves have contributed to it only from the turn of the century, but are now producing a definitive work under the auspices of the Nordic Lapp Institute. Even the most sympathetic and painstaking outsider can hardly provide the authenticity to be expected from native writers. Some accounts, particularly early ones, suffered from reflecting current intellectual fashions, partisan interests and even crack-pot theories, such as that identifying the Lapps with a lost tribe of Israel.

The earliest years

The first account we have of the Lapps is by the Roman historian, Tacitus, in his book on Germany (AD 98). He describes the Fenni, a hunting people 'extraordinarily wild and horribly poor', with bone-tipped weapons – 'their whole wealth is in arrows'. They have no horses, no houses, dress in furs, eat herbs and sleep on the ground. The women hunt with the men. Their sole shelter is 'some contraption of branches connected together'. In typical Silver Latin manner he then develops the 'noble savage' theme in implied criticism of the luxurious degeneracy of contemporary Rome. But his portrayal of Lapp life is basically correct: the vague phraseology of the reference to their shelters

– *aliquo nexu ramorum* – could even be a garbled description of their pole-tents. The Byzantine historian of the Gothic Wars, Procopius Caesariensis (*c* AD 550), who calls them Skrithiphinnoi, adds new details – the high mountains and forests with abundant game, the Lapp mother's habit of giving a marrow-bone to her baby to suck, and the use of a hanging cradle of skin. The name he uses, a version of the archaic Scandinavian *Skriðifinnōz* 'ski-running Lapps', also indicates, though he is apparently unaware of it, that they used skis; as, in fact, northern peoples had done for about 3,000 years. The first specific reference to skis, however, is a couple of hundred years later when Paulus Diaconus (Paul Warnefried) in his *History of the Lombards* (*c* 780) describes the Skritofinni as 'running on curved pieces of wood' in a land which has snow even in summer.

The Norsemen by this time knew the Lapps well. They had been moving into the southern part of their territory from the fourth century and sailing ever further up the coast. By the eighth century they had prosperous trading-posts as far east as Varanger. Unfortunately their literary genius did not foster systematic factual descriptions. Their many references to Lapps are incidental. Thus an old Icelandic formula for outlawing a truce-breaker drives him 'from God and God's Christendom as far as men chase wolves, Christians go to church . . . Lapps run on skis . . .'. In the sagas, however, two of the Lapps' main attributes are first mentioned, their skill as sorcerers and as shipbuilders. But it is tantalising to think how much the Norsemen might have contributed to our knowledge of the early Lapps.

The account given by the north Norwegian magnate, Ottar or Ohthere, to Alfred the Great of England and appended by him to his translation of Orosius *History of the World* (AD 892) well illustrates this. Ottar said he lived 'the farthest north of the Norsemen' near modern Tromsø (about 69°N). He set off in his ship to see how far the coast extended and whether anybody lived there. From his account he obviously sailed round the Kola Peninsula and well into the White Sea. All the way he saw 'fishermen, fowlers and hunters who were all Lapps'. In the east, however, a people he calls Biarms, who seemed to him to speak a version of the Lappish he knew from home, cultivated their land. At home he was one of the greatest men of the district, where most of his wealth came from taxes he levied on the Lapps in the form of skins, feathers, whales' teeth and hide-ropes. As well as the usual domestic cattle he owned 600 reindeer. Of these, six were valuable decoy reindeer which the Lapps used to capture wild ones.

It was many centuries before any comparable authoritative eyewitness description of the Lapps appeared. Meanwhile monkish chroniclers continued to record what was known and from time to time added new details. The first specific reference to the Lapp tent, for example, is by the Danish prelate, Saxo Grammaticus, in his monumental *Achievements of the Danes* (c 1208). 'Their house is not fixed', he says, and also mentions the Lapps' skill as archers and sorcerers. He, too, first uses the word Lapp in the name, Lappia, he gives their land. A hundred years later a Swedish document of 1328 first refers to the people as 'men commonly called Lapps' (Lappa).

By this time fundamental changes were already in train. The Norwegian settlement of the fjords was restricting the Lapps' old hunting grounds and compelling them also to turn to farming and cattle-breeding. Ottar's reference to the use of decoy reindeer shows that the first steps had been taken towards the animal's full domestication and the subsequent development of reindeer nomadism, as grazing grounds were settled and wild reindeer stocks depleted by over-hunting. The taxes he imposed on the Lapps and their work for him as reindeer-herders were further glimpses of a familiar future pattern. Christianity too was moving into Lapland, the first churches being built in the Troms district early in the thirteenth century. The Lapps' southern neighbours were now directing their official attention and resources northwards. A new phase in their history had begun.

The growth of central government

From the early fourteenth century the Swedish Crown began formally to assert the jurisdiction it had long vaguely claimed over its ill-defined Lapp territories. The crucial questions were land tenure and taxation. The Lapps required a great deal of land and untrammelled access to it to sustain their traditional life. By a proclamation of 1340 all such 'waste lands' were declared 'open to all'. True, for some time southern settlers had been moving in, but this public affirmation of their right to do so was a more serious matter. In addition it involved the right of individual ownership, which cut across the Lapps' communal holdings of each group's land and threatened their whole social structure.

The sweeping reforms of Gustav Vasa a century later brought more fundamental changes. He declared all uncultivated land and forests to be Crown property. He strengthened the State's role by appointing a new class of official, the Lapp sheriff (*Lappfogde*), whose main duties were to ensure that taxes, now increased and their base widened, were duly collected; to administer the law; and to supervise the king's reindeer. These measures led to the decline of the notorious 'Birkarls', so named probably because their original base was in the Pirkalla district of south Finland, though they have also been referred to Birkö at the head of Gulf of Bothnia. These well-organised freebooters, with their monopoly of trading with and collecting taxes from the Swedish Lapps, had exploited them from the early Middle Ages. They had divided the region among themselves into four districts – the Lappmarks (Lapp border districts) of Kemi, Torne, Lule and Pite. (For administrative reasons three others were formed later – Ume, Lycksele and Åsele.) In return for this lucrative business they paid a derisory tax to the Crown. At this time for the whole of the Pite and Lule Lapp districts, for example, they paid only 2 marten and 300 squirrel skins a year. After first doubling the Birkarls' contribution, the king in 1553 ruled that henceforth the Lapps should pay their taxes direct to the Crown, thereby removing a major source of the Birkarls' wealth and power. In this respect Gustav Vasa's reforms were to the Lapps advantage. His other measures were not.

The Lapps now became tenants of the Crown but had less security of tenure than the settlers, who were encroaching on their ancient preserves, because the establishment of a fixed dwelling with cultivated land created a right of ownership. When the inevitable disputes arose, the courts at first tended to support the Lapps. Even so it was only their right to use the land – the 'Lapp tax land' (*Lappskatteland*) – that was in question. They still could not own it. Towards the end of the seventeenth century, however, when the development of the North was an important part of national policy, the rules increasingly came to be interpreted in favour of the new immigrants. Under the famous 'Lappmark Edict' (*Lappmarksplakat*) of 1673, they were allowed to settle on Lapp tax land without the tenant's agreement. Eventually the payment of this tax gave the Lapp only the right to graze reindeer, to fish and to hunt on the land involved. Nor could this right, as earlier on, be inherited. It was extinguished by the death of the tenant and the authorities tended more and more to award a new tenancy not to the heir, but to a settler, on the grounds that farming was a more valuable use of the land than reindeer-herding and hunting.

The Lapps thus had to pay for the hunting and fishing which was vital to them. The settlers did not, but increasingly occupied themselves with these pursuits in a region so rich in game. This harmed the Lapps. Also, in the eyes of the central government, it ran counter to the whole policy of subsidising the development of the North in the best interests of the State. It thus became necessary to define the various parties' rights and to distinguish clearly between Crown lands and the land farmers had taken over (often Crown land). This was eventually done by drawing a boundary between 'Coast Land' and Lapp territory, the effective limit of which was the 'Lapp tax land' nearest the coast. Only Lapps and settlers on Crown land were to be allowed to hunt and fish on the latter and regulations to this effect, widely disregarded in practice, were published in 1751.

Other boundaries too were settled, and with more success, during this period. The frontier between Sweden – Finland and Russia was demarcated by the peace treaty of Tevsina in 1595. Under it a defeated Sweden relinquished all claims to the Kola Peninsula, which has ever since been part of Russia. Charles IX, however, partly to offset this loss, intensified Sweden's efforts in Lapland. He built forts on the Finnmark coast, churches further south. He granted to the Dutch, whom he settled in an enlarged Gothenburg, the right to fish off north Norway. He added 'King of the Kajans and the Lapps in the Lands of the North' to his other royal titles. These provocative actions annoyed Christian IV of Denmark – Norway and contributed to the outbreak of war between the two

28

countries in 1611. The great Finnmark fishery after all operated from Bergen in his kingdom; and Christian had no intention of allowing another ruler to control the northern route to Russia or to tax the Lapps in north Norway. Sweden lost the war and with it, in 1613, her foothold on the Arctic coast (and the extra royal title). It was not, however, until the Strömstad agreement of 1751 that the frontiers between the two kingdoms were properly delineated. The northern section later became the Norwegian boundary, first with Russia and now with Finland, but the line still remains as then drawn.

The territorial adjustments under this agreement were not particularly important. Norway gained the large parishes of Kautokeino and Karasjok, today the heart of Norwegian Lapland; Sweden two parishes in Dalecarlia. Juridically, however, it marked a milestone in Lapp affairs and hence is often described as the Lapps' Magna Charta. In two codicils annexed to it the nomadic Lapps were granted the right to move their reindeer freely between the two countries on their spring and autumn migrations, without regard to the frontier even in time of war. Other rights and responsibilities were defined in a manner unusually enlightened for the age. In particular it was agreed that the same Lapps should no longer be taxed by more than one country. Some in north Finland had long paid taxes to Sweden, Norway and Russia: and Russia continued where possible to double-tax them well into the nineteenth century after she had acquired Finland from Sweden.

The age of discovery

The negotiators of the Strömstad agreement had been greatly helped by the comprehensive and perspicacious report on conditions in Lapland prepared for them by a Norwegian officer, Major Peter Schnitler. He particularly emphasised the reindeer nomad's absolute need of different seasonal grazing-grounds, and the fact that the above-mentioned codicil takes legal cognisance of this is generally placed to his credit. In general, however, there was by this time no lack of information on Lapland. The

2   (overleaf) Carta Marina of Olaus Magnus, 1539 (Royal Library, Stockholm)

ROS MARVS PISCIS

E

STAPPEN

DOMVS
PRESIDII
LAS OLAVI

VAR
DAHVS

MALKVR

SEVTTOBERG
FIND
BOMGANG

SAMAVIK

DOMS HAP

VILDAL

HONAVIE

REDELVIK ROTELVIK

FINMARCHIA

GERVLD

HELGANES

TETA
BORG

TELAV

AVVER

LAD BIRO

NDVAD

GREX RAGI
FERORVM

BERKARA
QVENAP

MINTA
AVRI

I

LAPPIA

CAPITANEI

OCCIDENTALIS

BIRCARORVM

SIDREM

K

VLVLA

K

MINTA

BIRCARL

GVLO
NES

G

SKEL
LITTA

H

MARE

ABBI
SKIRA

BENSIN

previous two centuries indeed can aptly be described as the age of its discovery.

Two Swedish Catholic priests, the Månsson brothers – or, in the Latin which brought them fame, Johannes and Olaus Magnus – who chose exile in Rome rather than the Reformation in their native land, produced the first, and in some experts' opinion the most important, major works specifically about the Lapps. (The first book devoted to the subject was in fact German – Jacob Ziegler's, *Schondia* (1532), but his information came mainly from Johannes Magnus, whose own book later appeared posthumously). In 1539 Olaus Magnus published his *Carta Marina*, a map of Fennoscandia with many illustrations and informative notes. His sometimes fanciful, but often accurate, portrayal of a northern wonderland made an enormous impact on contemporary Europe, which his great *History of the Peoples of the North* (1555) reinforced.

A Norwegian clergyman, Peder Claussøn Friis, made the next significant contribution with his *Description of Norway and adjacent Islands* (1632). His account of the Sea Lapps is particularly valuable. Further information is found in other works of the period, but it is piecemeal. The appearance in Frankfurt in 1673 of Johan Scheffer's *Lapponia*, an

3   Two Lapps and a pack-reindeer (*Scheffer, Bodleian Library*)

4 Mountain Lapps from Karasjok, from J.A. Friis, *Lappisk Mythologi*, 1871 (*Dr E.J. Lindgren-Utsi*)

invaluable monograph dealing with all aspects of Lapp life, was a very different matter. It was commissioned by the Chancellor of Sweden to provide the fullest possible survey of a region of growing importance to the State. Scheffer, an Alsatian, was Professor of Rhetoric and Politics at Uppsala and in fact never visited Lapland. In addition to all known historical sources he relied on the excellent reports that clergymen well acquainted with the people and the region were officially required to produce for him. (The most important contributions, which were published separately in full a few years ago, were by Samuel Rheen, Olaus Petrus Niurenius, and Johannes Tornaeus). With its excellent maps and splendid illustrations the book aroused enormous interest, particularly in England, and remains a standard work.

The increase in Norwegian activity in Lapland about this time produced further information, of which the Regional Governor, Hans

Lilienskiold's, *Mirror of the North* (1698) and the missionary, Thomas von Westen's, *Topographia Ecclesiastica* (1717), are good examples. In Sweden the young Linnaeus wrote a diary of his visit to Lapland in 1732, full of precise observations and astute comments. The first systematic book based on residence among the Lapps appeared soon afterwards when Per Högström, the first rector of Gällivare, published his *Description of the Lappmarks of the Swedish Crown* (1747). Within a few years another major work came out in Norway, again by a clergyman, Knud Leem, headmaster and teacher of Lappish in the Lapp Seminary at Trondheim. This was his *Description of the Lapps of Finnmark* (1767). No longer were the Lapps the little known, remote, people of previous ages.

Spread of Christianity

From the early eleventh century the preaching of Christianity was a major factor in changing the Lapps' way of life, both in itself and through the secular teaching of which it was the official instrument. Early Norwegian kings, notably St Olav in 1020, first spread the Gospel in the north. Their successors slowly continued the process; by 1308 there was a church as far along the coast as Vardø. By this time the Swedes, whose first missionary to the Lapps had been Stenfi (c 1050), were also making a more purposeful effort, with Torneå (Tornio), where a church was dedicated in 1345, as the main centre of their activities. To judge, however, from the journey the famous Lapp Christian woman, Margareta, made some fifty years later as far south as Lund to petition the Swedish queen to increase the Church's work among her heathen countrymen, there was much backsliding. Since many Lappish words for aspects of the Christian faith are of Russian origin, it is probable that at this earlier period the Orthodox Church made a bigger and more successful contribution than the record indicates. The first accounts of its missionary activities in fact date only from the sixteenth century when, at the Lapps' own request, a monastery was established at Kola in 1527. In 1530 the redoubtable Trifon, subsequently sanctified, founded the great monastery at Patsjanga (Petsamo). By the end of the century the Orthodox faith had been carried as far west as Varanger

34

Fjord, one energetic priest somewhat improbably claiming to have 'converted' 2,000 Lapps in one day.

Given the ambitions of the northern states at this time, these developments were as much political and territorial as religious. The Norwegians steadily consolidated their influence and, in the late sixteenth century, had seventeen churches in Finnmark. Christian IV took a personal interest in rooting out the old Lapp religion and, in 1609, imposed (without much effect) the death penalty for sorcery, largely because he attributed to Lapp spells the near fatal dangers of a voyage he had made along the north coast. His rival, Charles IX of Sweden, in 1603 decreed the building of churches in main Lapp centres such as Arvidsjaur, Lycksle, Jokkmokk and Enontekis (Enontekiö). Lapp boys were selected for training as priests and the famous Skyttean School was opened at Lycksele in 1632 on the initiative of Johan Skytte, formerly the king's tutor.

There was meanwhile a lull in missionary activity in Norway, partly because the Lutheran, unlike the Roman Catholic, Church was not as a matter of doctrine a crusading Church. However, a new and final phase in the conversion of the Lapps began around the turn of the century. The first church specifically for Lapps was built at Varanger under a royal decree of 1691. Soon afterwards the energetic and fanatical Thomas von Westen, 'the Apostle of the Lapps', began an effective onslaught on their old religion. He founded the Lapp Seminary at Trondheim, built other schools and more churches and established an effective ecclesiastical administration. His successors continued the work. By the end of the eighteenth century the Christian faith was widely and firmly established in Lapland.

The somewhat arid forms of official Lutheranism and its limited concept of an individual relationship with the Deity did not, however, satisfy the Lapps. They were also under pressure from new economic and social developments injurious to their traditional life. A new revivalist cult arose on the mid-1800s and spread rapidly. It appealed to the cathartic group ecstasy of the old religion as well as inspiring a moral rebirth in an increasingly materialistic and sinful world. This was Laestadianism which, from 1845 onwards, sprang from the powerful preaching of Lars Levi Laestadius, the Pastor of Karesuando. Unfortunately the ecstasy of group communion (*likkatus*) sometimes turned to mob frenzy, as in the fatal riots in Kautokeino in 1852. But the new doctrine, now moderated, retains an essential role in the Lutheran religion as practised by the Lapps, not least because it helps to preserve the old values and the traditional social structure.

The introduction of education

In the northern, as in other, states the Church was long officially responsible for education. To operate effectively missionaries in Lapland had both to enlighten their parishioners and to learn the local language themselves. Hence the first books in Lappish – a simple ABC catechism and a short hymnal in 1619 – were of a religious nature. Equally, as noted above, clergymen were responsible for most of the first detailed accounts of Lapland. Modern educational facilities for the Lapps are described later (p 141), but the early efforts of the Church, which took different forms in the three countries, deserve mention here.

Norwegian policy on Lapp education has vacillated since the early eighteenth century between teaching the Lapps as a recognised minority in their own language and using the schools to turn them into Norwegians. Before then the problem was a simpler one of converting them to Christianity, which the missionaries best achieved by instructing them in Lappish. The spread of education coincided, particularly in the last century, with both the rise of Norwegian nationalism and the acceptance of theories of cultural evolution which required 'primitive peoples' to be improved. The growth of industry put the Lapps at a further disadvantage. As Professor Gutorm Gjessing aptly remarks in his *Changing Lapps* (1954), 'a people without factories could obviously not be a people of culture'. Culture was to be brought to them through their absorption by the modern Norwegian society.

Thus, although there was a steady improvement in the educational facilities available to the Lapps from the 1850s, it was accompanied by the decline in the use of their language in schools. In 1880 it was banned by the Troms County Council except for religious instruction, six years later by the Norwegian parliament. The country's mood at the time of the dissolution of the union with Sweden engendered an energetic policy of Norwegianisation in the decades around 1900. Again the material conditions were, as a result, improved. Boarding-schools, for example, were built. In the words of the administrator responsible they were, however, conceived as one of the most useful tools in the above policy. As recently as 1936 the ban on Lappish for non-religious instruction was confirmed by law. In fact, though relaxed for primary instruction in 1959, it was in force until 1969. The full rigours of this policy, however, were softened by the activities of the Norwegian Mission to the Lapps, which since its foundation in 1888 has played an important role in general, as well as religious, education.

The Swedes' approach to the education of the Lapps was more consistent, though long affected by a paternalism which aimed at meeting what they, rather than the Lapps, considered their special requirements. Hence, somewhat surprisingly, the material facilities provided in Sweden until quite recently lagged behind those in Norway in the interests of not 'making the children unused to nomad life'. At least the intention was good. All the same, in addition to the Skyttean School mentioned above, which was already sending Lapps to Uppsala University, there were by the early eighteenth century seven permanent schools at Lapp winter settlements. In 1735 travelling schools ('catachete schools') were introduced. They provided the rudiments of literacy and Christian religion as the teachers moved round to the different nomad encampments. In 1818 the number of permanent schools was reduced to three, which were incorporated in the ordinary Swedish primary system, and that of the catachete schools increased to twenty-seven. They were abolished towards the end of the century – a dark period in Lapp education in Sweden – without anything replacing them. Also, about 1870, Lappish ceased to be used to teach Lapp children.

Travelling nomad schools (kåtaskolor, 'tent-schools'), were revived by a law of 1913. They functioned for twenty-eight weeks a year for each group visited. Older children spent three months a year in boarding-school over a period of three years. As these changes were implemented they aroused strong criticism. The travelling schools gave a manifestly inadequate education. The boarding-schools consisted of tents and turf-huts, again to avoid 'spoiling the pupils for the hard life of a nomad'. At a special meeting in 1918 the Lapp National Council demanded the abolition of travelling schools and the provision of proper boarding accommodation. Neither was achieved until over twenty years later. Thereafter Lapp education, as well as having certain special features, has steadily been brought into step with standard Swedish practice.

In Finland and Russia until after World War I educational facilities for Lapps were slight. At the beginning of this century only one Kola Lapp in a hundred could read. After the Bolshevik Revolution 'Red Tent' propaganda teams spread their particular brand of enlightenment in the 1920s. The basis of more systematic education was provided in the next decade. Lapp teachers were trained at the new Northern Institute at Leningrad and the Murmansk Polytechnic. The local Lappish was written for the first time. Primary schools were expanded, using Lappish for teaching. This has now been replaced by Russian, but remains in use at a later stage in boarding-schools. Since independence, Finland has given the Lapps the same educational opportunities as its other citizens, with their special needs met under the liberal provisions which the constitution of 1919 lays down for minorities. Instruction is in Lappish, normally by Lapps, and there is a full range of excellent schools, many providing residential accommodation.

Towards the modern economy

From the mid-sixteenth to the mid-twentieth century Lapland progressed towards its modern economy, with all the manifold consequences of such change. Both pace and emphasis differed in different regions. But, in addition to the factors mentioned above, there were certain common ones – changes in reindeer-management and migration, the demands and the disturbances of war, a general similarity of resources, the stresses of industrialisation and the machine age, the effect of improved communications and the virtual replacement of a subsistence by a cash economy. As usual in such cultural conflicts, contemporary evidence tends to be contradictory and, in both senses, partial. Casual references, rather than the main theme of lengthy accounts, and artefacts still extant provide valuable correctives. For example, whatever their contemporary detractors stated, the amount of silverware the Sea Lapps have left from the eighteenth century is tangible proof that they were then prosperous and, therefore, reasonably efficient and industrious. Only mining in Swedish Lapland is extensively documented from its earliest days, Professor Gunnar Ahlström's stylish and informative *The Dark Mountain* (1966) being the latest general account. But the main features of this period of vital economic change are noted below.

On balance the Sea Lapps of north Norway, prior to the advent of machines, fared better than both other Lapps and, in fact, than the Norwegians in their territory. The Norwegians of Finnmark were not allowed to own land until 1775. They were transient. Their numbers fluctuated greatly. They were less efficient than the Lapps in wresting a living from a harsh climate and a special region. They were permitted to trade only with, and were chronically in debt to, the merchant monopolies of Bergen. The Lapps, by contrast, were expert boat-builders, fishermen and sealers with a practically self-sufficient economy, diversified by lucrative barter with Russians, whose ships came to the fjords each summer in the 'Pomor trade' which started in 1742 and ended only with World War I. From the mid-nineteenth century, however, the Lapps' relative position worsened as new methods and machines, for which they had neither the education nor the capital to exploit, were introduced. It is only since the massive post-war reconstruction of the area that, with the influx of new money and new attitudes from Oslo, it has taken a turn for the better.

Economic developments in Swedish Lapland, starting with mining in the seventeenth century, have profoundly affected the Lapps' traditional life. Silver was the first metal mined in 1634, near Arjeplog (where there is a fascinating Silver Museum). Hopes of an 'Arctic Peru' were disappointed, partly because the Lapps forced to work there were so badly treated that they just decamped; but some silver continued to be produced. The first successful venture into iron-mining was in 1643 and the famous Kengis works were opened three years later by Grape. A more ambitious scheme at Svappavara by the Momma family a little later did not see the century out. Early in the eighteenth century the rich deposits in the Gällivare district, which Lapps had shown to prospectors, began to be worked. As the industrial revolution in Western Europe stimulated demand, the Gellivare Company was floated in London in 1864. In 1902 it completed the railway to the ice-free Norwegian port of Narvik. Taken over by the Swedish state in 1907, it has, as the Luossavara-Kirunavara Company, been of great economic importance both to Lapland and western Europe. This railway, incidentally, provides an early illustration of the effect of modern communication on the Lapps. It follows the line of an ancient Lapp migratory trail and, with better gradients and a wider track, has replaced it.

The forest industry was meanwhile moving north making further inroads into Lapp lands and life. The establishment in 1869 of a visibly demarcated boundary (*odlingsgräns*, 'the boundary of cultivation') between Lapp and other territory, no farming being allowed above it, had only partially prevented this. But, since the establishment in 1910 of the first northern hydro-electric station at Porjus, near Jokkmokk, it has been the Swedish state itself which has systematically destroyed old grazing and calving grounds by flooding valleys to provide water for ever more generating stations. Fishing, both subsistence and commercial, has been crippled, or destroyed, in many lakes. The 'Lappfund' pays agreed sums in compensation, but cash cannot replace a lost environment. Similarly, tourism began to make a significant contribution to Lapland's economy early this century. Inevitably the numbers of people attracted and the facilities provided – roads, paths, hotels – have tended to disturb traditional life.

Finnish Lapland moved towards its modern economy in a simpler manner. The Scandinavian wars of the early eighteenth century accelerated the long-standing, but slight, shift of Finnish settlers to the north. Difficult times subsequently brought new influxes. In the Napoleonic era accounts speak of 'beggars with swollen faces who could neither sit nor stand' on the road north. The depression of the 1860s caused further immigration. To provide themselves with farms these new arrivals burnt the forests. Thus, in contrast to Norway and Sweden, they did not compete with the Lapps for land; they simply changed its nature so completely that it could no longer serve the Lapps' traditional activities.

Some Lapps took to farming, while many settlers became reindeer-breeders, introducing new co-operative methods which the Lapps also have adopted. Forestry, too, played a part in the change, as did mining, the most important enterprise being the nickel mine near Petsamo, now ceded to the Soviet Union. As in Norway, the present phase of development began with the post-war reconstruction of a devastated region.

The English connection

Of the peoples outside Scandinavia, the English have throughout the years shown the greatest interest in Lapland. The early story of this long connection is worth describing. In terms of their written contribution to our knowledge of the region it begins, apart from Alfred's *History*, with the Elizabethan merchant adventurers. The Arctic attracted them for two reasons: they hoped to find a North-East Passage to the riches of Asia; they wanted to trade with Russia free of the irksome Danish control of the entrance to the Baltic. We thus find them off the north coast of Lapland by the middle of the sixteenth century. The first known list of Lappish words was produced in 1557 by an English merchant, Stephen Burrough. Through their base at Archangel these traders established good local connections and thus provide us, from Russian sources, with useful details of the Kola Lapps of the period. These they call 'Lappians' who 'will say that they beleeve in the Russes' God'. The Norwegian Sea Lapps they speak of as 'Scrickfinnes, who neither know God nor yet good order'.

The publication of Scheffer's book prompted another upsurge of English interest in Lapland at the end of the seventeenth century. An English translation appeared in 1674, the year after the original Latin version. The Royal Society made much of it, devoting considerable space to the subject in its publications. It was skilfully plagiarised in the commentary to the sumptuous and widely sold *The English Atlas* in 1680. Daniel Defoe wrote an unsuccessful book, *The Life and Adventures of Duncan Campbell*, in the style of *Robinson Crusoe* about the son of a ship-wrecked Scotsman and the beautiful daughter of a rich Lapp. Addison published poems about reindeer in *The Spectator*. The fashionable poet,

James Thomson, gave an idyllic account of Lapp life in *The Seasons*, and the first of many personal accounts of travels in Lapland by the English appeared in 1724 in Aubry de la Mottraye's *Travels through Europe, Asia and into Part of Africa*.

The last phase of what might be called the English discovery of Lapland was ushered in towards the end of the century when Sir Henry St George Liddell took a trip to Lapland for a wager. He brought back several reindeer and two girls in national costume. Their appearance awakened lively public interest; and the tour itself was described by Mathew Consett in a book published in 1789 with disappointing illustrations by Thomas Bewick. In 1821 the enterprising owner of the new public exhibition rooms in London, the Egyptian Hall, staged a highly successful Lapp exhibition with an Arctic panorama, reindeer, real Lapps and all, which Rowlandson and Cruikshank recorded. The Anglicised Italian, Joseph Acerbi, had meanwhile (1802) produced an engaging, but not wholly authentic, account of his travels in the region. Others, more expert and specialised, such as the Professor of Geology at Cambridge, Edward Clarke, were also now taking professional interest in the region. As the industrial revolution subsequently gathered pace, it was the turn of the entrepreneur who came to develop, not to study, Lapland.

3

THE REINDEER

The reindeer, wild or tame, has been crucial to the survival of the Lapps throughout history and is the basis of the unique monoculture which is their traditional life in the eyes of the world. Yet the reindeer nomadism which this generally connotes is both a comparatively recent development and has never been practised by the majority. It is now seldom practised and, since the introduction in the 1950s of improved mechanical transport, only in a manner far different from the earlier treks with skis and reindeer-trains. Economic and social developments too have militated against it. The reindeer is still a major asset to the Lapps, but their ways of exploiting it have had to change to something more in step with modern requirements; and are changing still. Nevertheless, the age-old and intimate association of the Lapps and their reindeer has been of such paramount importance to every aspect of their culture and their character, and is in any case so intrinsically interesting, that any account of the Lapps must give it priority.

General description and attributes

The reindeer (the North American caribou) belongs to a family of Arctic deer which, despite variations in size, weight and habitat, most authorities consider one species, *Rangifer tarandus*. The Mountain Lapps' animals are smaller than those of the Forest Lapps. They are not as big as most outsiders expect, partly because the male's antlers give a misleading impression of their actual size. They stand $2\frac{1}{2}$ to 3ft (about 1m) high.

Their weight varies greatly. Males are heavier than females: a big male may weigh up to 400lb (180kg), but about 250lb (113kg) is more usual. They are strong and very hardy but, away from their normally germ-free surroundings, dangerously susceptible to several diseases. The domesticated breed is sensitive, docile when trained, and attractive. Their coats are normally greyish-fawn, though colours range from creamy-white to near black with a great variety of local markings. Young calves are usually reddish-brown. These differences in colour, combined with qualities such as age (in eight stages up to $6\frac{1}{2}$ years), sexual state (calf; bull, intact or gelded; cow, fertile, pregnant, sterile) and antler formation, have been utilised by the Lapps to create a remarkable classification system which can provide thousands of combinations and enables each animal to be identified accurately and immediately. Only the Bedouin have any comparable, but much less developed, method for describing their camels.

5　Lasso training (*John Savio*)

44

6 and 7 (*above*) Young reindeer bull; (*below*) Wolves and reindeer (*John Savio*)

The reindeer is the only deer of which both sexes grow antlers, including the forward-projecting brow-tine. It has a well developed herd instinct. In good conditions the hinds are very fertile, nine out of ten usually producing one calf each year from their second to their tenth year. They are then often slaughtered because their teeth become too worn for them to feed properly and produce healthy calves. The annual increase may amount to up to 40 per cent of the whole herd, which enables the occasional catastrophic losses in bad years to be rapidly made good. Mating takes place over a period of about two weeks in October, calves are born from late April to early June, for which purpose the hinds seek out snow-free patches of ground on the lower mountain slopes, usually the same year after year. In managed herds the best bulls are selected in late summer for breeding; the others are gelded (traditionally by a man's teeth through a piece of cloth). The most intelligent are trained as draught animals. The others are slaughtered in autumn or winter according to need and the wholesalers' requirements. When in rut, the bulls are extremely aggressive and particularly resent any interference with their harem.

The main food of the reindeer is 'reindeer moss' and many species of plants, with marked seasonal variations. While there is snow on the ground they live on lichens (p 16) and can dig through about 3ft (1m) of snow. With the thaw they roam widely to get grasses and young plant shoots. Birch and willow-leaves are much relished, but they do not touch conifers. In the autumn they eat as many fungi as they can.

Several of the reindeer's enemies, including certain flies, have already been mentioned (p 15). The most hated is the wolf, which is more mobile than the reindeer. Wolves hunt in packs and attack at night. The herd panics and scatters when it smells the wolves, which may kill large numbers from sheer blood-lust. Turi, a wolf-hunter by profession, states that he has known one wolf kill ten reindeer. The wolverine creeps up on reindeer when they have their heads down feeding in the snow and bites through the neck. It hunts alone and it also is a wanton killer. Bears kill reindeer only occasionally. They cannot overtake them and, in any case, are primarily vegetarians.

The main diseases to which reindeer are subject are hoof-rot and intestinal infections (tapeworms), which may spread rapidly in a herd. They are also subject to vertigo and lumbar paralysis. Anthrax, known as Siberian reindeer pest, has now been extirpated. It is worth noting that there are still large numbers of wild reindeer in central Norway and some in north Sweden. In Finland many domesticated reindeer have reverted to the wild state.

Reindeer products

Every part of a reindeer can be used for food, clothing, tools or other products. Its milk is extremely rich, though only about a quarter of a pint is produced at a time. It contains 20 per cent fat, 10 per cent protein and 4 per cent milk-sugar. Corresponding figures for cow's milk are 3.7, 3.6 and 4.6 per cent. It is used fresh in coffee or preserved as cheese or curdled. The hinds lactate at five different periods of from two to six weeks, from the time they calve in May up to early November. They are therefore milked at different stages of the nomad's seasonal migration and in different circumstances; the whole time-consuming process became an important aspect of traditional nomadic life. The meat, fresh or preserved, is excellent, not least because, so far as possible, it is obtained from selected animals when they are in their prime (from 4 to 5 years) not, as with venison from wild deer, when the hunter is able to bag his quarry. It is comparatively lean and unusually rich in protein and important vitamins. The tongue and marrow-bones are delicacies. The blood is used for gruel, pancakes and sausages. Other parts are eaten fresh or preserved. The animal's own stomach is cleaned and used to store food. Its intestines serve as sausage casings. One animal produces from about 90 to 140lb (40–64kg) of meat.

The pelt provides the finest natural cold-weather clothing available. It is still widely used as such throughout the Arctic and is indispensable for bedding and groundsheets. The dressed hide is made into other garments – leggings, tunics, boots. The bones are made into knife-handles, sheaths, buttons and other small objects. The sinews are traditionally used in the construction of things like sledges or panniers, and for sewing leather objects. They may also be stranded to make a strong thread.

Reindeer are normally slaughtered in the winter when the flesh is at its best, especially in early winter after a summer of rich grazing. By law, modern abattoirs with humane killers must now be used, if the meat is to be sold wholesale. But traditional methods of individual slaughtering by a knife, considered to give a better-flavoured meat, are used for private consumption. The northern Lapps originally used a single stab to the heart, the southern Lapps a double stab, the first in the back of the head to stun the animal before the death-blow. This latter method has long been in general use. In both the knife was retained in the body for some time to prevent the blood running to waste.

Ancient hunting

The most striking aspect of the hunting of wild reindeer of old is the sheer size of the herds. Both eye-witness accounts and, more impressively, the remains of earlier vast trapping systems, bear witness to this. The Lapps, women as well as men, hunted and were particularly skilled in pursuing their quarry on skis. Decoy reindeer, as Ottar's account (p 25) shows, were used to entice wild reindeer within range at least as early as the ninth century. Several hundred years later, at any rate, the hunter often hid behind the decoy and shot through its antlers. Noose-snares (Illus. 8) were concealed in trees, or in gaps in crude fences, with bows and arrows and, later, guns, set off by a trip-line. Such contrivances were used well into the nineteenth century. But the most remarkable and productive methods, remains of which are found all

8   Noose-snare (*after W. von Wright, 1832*)

over Lapland at suitable sites, were pitfalls and stockades.

Lines of pitfalls were dug along the reindeers' migratory track in places such as narrow valleys or tongues of firm land in lakes and marshes which limited their freedom of manoeuvre. This was further restricted by building fences parallel to the line of movement. All the pits are oval. Their original dimensions varied from 7 to 10ft (2 to 3m) long, 4 to 7ft (1–2m) broad and 4 to 6ft (1–2m) deep. Their sides were steep to prevent the trapped animal climbing out and were sometimes lined with several layers of flat stones on edge to deny its hooves purchase. No pits have been found with sharpened stakes, pointed stones or spear-heads

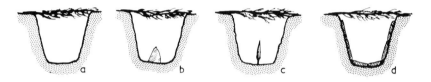

9   Pitfalls: a) usual type; b) pointed stone; c) spike; d) smooth stone lining (*after Vorren*)

fixed at the bottom, although early writers refer to such devices. The distance between pits varies from about 1yd (1m) to well over 100yd (90m). The hole at the top was carefully concealed by a covering of twigs with peat, leaves, moss and so on above it.

Many such systems have been investigated in recent decades, notably by Professor Ørnulv Vorren in the Varanger district and Professor Ernst Manker in north Sweden. Research up to that time is comprehensively described in Manker's *Fångstgropar och Stalotomter* (1960) (Trapping Pits and 'Stalo sites'). Thousands of examples are known and many are very extensive. That at Gollevarre, for example, in a valley between the head of Varanger Fjord and the Tana River, has 15 separate groups of pitfalls with 2,426 pits, the biggest having 550 pitfalls over a distance of 5 miles (8km). Other big systems are near Karasjok, in the wooded country between the big rivers of north Sweden behind Skellefteå, and Umeå, and near Lake Inari in Finland. Radioactive dating has shown that some are

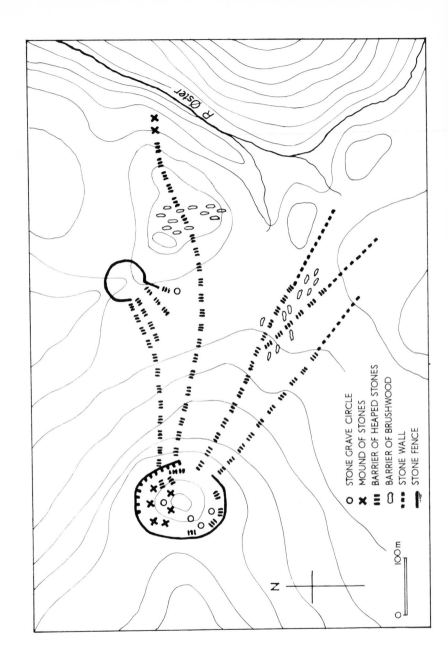

R Öster

STONE GRAVE CIRCLE
MOUND OF STONES
BARRIER OF HEAPED STONES
BARRIER OF BRUSHWOOD
STONE WALL
STONE FENCE

N

100 m

as old as the eighth century. Many systems contain an ancient sacrificial site, where offerings were doubtless made in the hope of, or in gratitude for, a successful hunt. Larger shallower depressions with a low encircling wall are found on, or near, many sites. They are popularly described as 'Stalo sites' – places where the giant of Lapp mythology, Stalo, lived. But they are clearly remains of ancient settlements.

The other important trapping method was the stockade, or corral (*vuobma*), of which many descriptions are found from the mid-seventeenth century onwards; in a modified form it is still used in some places to round up tame herds. One type consisted of two fences from 3 to 6 miles (4–9km) long and up to 6 miles (10km) apart at the open end on fairly level ground, but converging at the other to a circular enclosure or a blind slope below a crag. The fence at the open end consisted of fairly short poles 'with something black on top' (probably fluttering rags or an intimidating lump of peat) to keep the reindeer on course. At the other end the poles were taller and closer together in the form of a

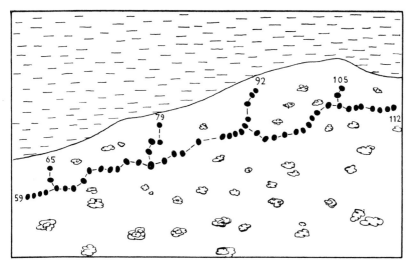

11   Part of the Gollevarre pitfall system on the shore of Lake Korsmyra below Julelvmoen Hill (*after Vorren*)

proper stockade. The animals were driven into the trap by a line of men and dogs and either killed, or captured for taming, in the dead end. One such hunt in Finland in the seventeenth century is said to have accounted for 1,000 animals in a day. Even allowing for exaggeration, such an account illustrates what an amazing abundance of wild reindeer there once was.

This form of hunting was practised at two seasons: from mid-September to early November and from about 20 March until the ground was bare of snow. Excessive hunting, coupled with the steady encroachment of Scandinavian settlers on the old hunting-grounds, led to serious depletion of the wild herds. From the sixteenth century onwards the Mountain Lapps began to rely more and more on their herds of tame animals, to manage which they developed the full reindeer nomadism which until quite recently has been typical of their life.

Reindeer nomadism

By nomadism is meant that culture whose chief characteristic is that groups of people accompany on their seasonal migrations the more or less domesticated herds of the particular animal which is the basis of their existence. For the Lapps that animal is the reindeer and they practise reindeer nomadism. The origins of this system have been debated since the mid-1800s, two main, but opposed, theories emerging early this century – the diffusion theory and the evolution theory. The diffusionists hold that reindeer-herding originated in eastern Asia round Lake Baikal, where it is first mentioned in Chinese annals of the fifth century, and subsequently spread elsewhere. The evolutionists contend that, whether there happen to be written records or not, it was a natural development in many separate places among hunting peoples who were in close contact with the reindeer and came to see the advantages of taming it, as happened with other animals now domesticated. Opinion now favours the evolutionary theory, since various stages of the development of reindeer management up to, and including, full nomadism are still found among Lapps and other reindeer peoples whose circumstances have not compelled them to take this final step. The Forest Lapps practise 'half-nomadism' with only short migrations in the vicinity of their homes. Some Skolt Lapps have domesticated reindeer which never leave their crofts.

A further distinction is also made between intensive and extensive nomadism. The former describes the Forest Lapps' methods and involves strict control of the animals, which are used for milk, meat, skins and as draught animals. Extensive nomadism implies that the reindeer are scarcely herded for long periods of the year, that they make long migrations and are exploited primarily for their meat and hides. One of its characteristic features is the periodic round-up. As Professor Robert Paine points out, however, in his paper on 'The Herd Management of Lapp Reindeer Pastoralists', the proper management of either an intensive or an extensive herd is much more complicated than these neat distinctions assume and in their detailed operation the two methods to a large extent overlap.

The unique features of extensive nomadism which distinguish what is popularly regarded as the quintessential Lapp culture are described briefly below. It was developed by the northern Lapps and introduced by them to southern districts. This occurred particularly in the 1920s. Important changes were then made to the original agreement on frontiers which had been concluded in 1905, when Norway became independent. These seriously restricted the Lapps' former free movement from Sweden into their traditional grazing grounds and led many northern Lapps, who could no longer cross to Norwegian pastures, to move further south in Sweden.

The decisive factors in the now dominant northern Lapp system of reindeer management are terrain in terms of pasture and weather in terms of snow. In response to changes in both it involves seasonal migration in spring and autumn of up to 250 miles, a typical distance being

12 (overleaf) The Swedish Lapps have two main traditions: the Forest Lapps who live by agriculture and intensive reindeer breeding in the lower regions all year round, and the Mountain Lapps who live only by reindeer breeding, alternating between the mountain in summer and the forest in winter. The round-ups are a fine spectacle. Nowadays the deer are mostly driven by men riding on snow scooters (*Swedish Tourist Traffic Association*)

about 150 miles. The traditional routes follow well-known trails through mountains and, in the winter, across frozen lakes. Streams are forded, rivers and wider expanses of water crossed by boat, with the leading reindeer towed behind for the others to follow. The animals are good swimmers and their hollow hair helps to keep them afloat. Each Lapp group – the *siida* (p 64) – consists of from 10 to perhaps 90 persons in from 2 to 6 families with from 160 to 3,500 reindeer. Journeys are completed in 10 to 15 stages, stops being made at regular sites where huts, storehouses and useful implements are left from year to year. Tents are used both for short stops and often at the summer encampment. In the final stages of the return in the autumn, and elsewhere depending on

13   Reindeer marks: a = grandfather, younger son, youngest grandson. Other members of the family have their own variations of the basic mark which always passes to the youngest son

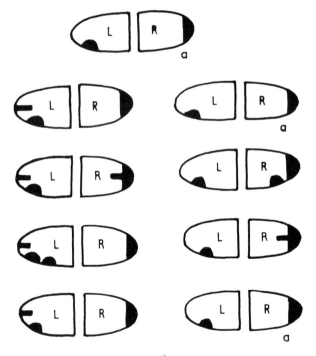

circumstances, there are also long-standing arrangements for families to stay on farms. The close relationships thus established are an important feature of traditional society.

This whole subject of nomadism is exhaustively treated in Manker's 'The Nomadism of the Swedish Mountain Lapps in 1945' and much more briefly, but from the inside, in the only account in English by a Lapp, 'The Reindeer-Breeding Methods of the Northern Lapps', by Mikel Utsi. The reindeer nomads' year begins with the first signs of thaw when the reindeer begin to move out from winter quarters to be at the calving grounds in May. The pregnant hinds are here kept separate and carefully tended. About mid-June, when the youngest calves are a fortnight or so old, the whole herd moves to lusher summer pastures and fly-free mountain slopes. The warm coast of northern Norway and its outlying islands with cool, healthy, breezes are ideal for calving and summer-grazing. Those who have made the long trek there recall with delight the thrill of the last night on top of the watershed before the mad rush down into Norway as the deer smell the warmer air and fresh pasture.

June is also the time for putting owners' marks on the new calves, using a distinctive and hereditary pattern of nicks on the ear, capable of endless variations (Illus. 13). These marks must be registered and are protected by law.

Traditionally the cows were first milked now, an ingenious muzzle being put on the calf to prevent it getting all the milk. Each route had its set milking stations. Men and women collaborated in this slow and burdensome task, the man holding the cow, the woman milking it into a distinctive scoop. For many years, however, milking has been discontinued at several of the possible seasons, since regular supplies of cow's or goat's milk, as well as of tinned milk, have become available. At these round-ups, as at other times, the Lapps make effective use of their lasso, the handling of which they practise from childhood.

In September the trek back begins to the autumn encampment to supervise the rutting season in October. Males not selected for breeding are gelded for later slaughter and a few are chosen as draught animals or as herd-leaders; the shape of the head and configuration of the antlers indicate to the expert an animal's suitability for this latter role. At the end of November the herd moves down to winter quarters in wooden houses, the early examples, as at Arvidsjaur, being small with sloping walls like a tent. The slaughter of suitable animals both for sale and family consumption, which began at the autumn camp, continues at intervals until the early spring when the summer supply is prepared and smoked.

The Mountain Lapps on the move, especially over sunlit snow, are a breathtaking, unforgettable, sight which has justifiably captured the imagination of the world. The co-ordination between man and beast, the fluid movement of the whole caravan, or train (*raid*, *rai'to*), provide a beautiful example of a highly specialised culture, whether in the management of the reindeer or the design of clothes, tents and other implements. It is all too easy to forget the long, cold, winters, the steady

14 Mountain Laplanders returning into the interior at the close of summer (*Brooke, Bodleian Library*)

15   Pannier for pack-reindeer

exertion and the strain of constant watchfulness.

Two groups are involved in such migrations, usually moving separately – the herds and the households. The herds are led by a trained and trusty ox and a man, and most of the animals are content to follow. The less tractable are kept in the herd by other men and dogs – 'the Lapp's most faithful servant'. The dogs are a type of Pomeranian. They are well, but firmly, treated, like other members of the family and, when old, are often killed to avoid an uncomfortable old age. With the ski and the lasso they constitute the reindeer-herder's essential tools.

The family train consists of about nine reindeer (including an unladen reserve) in single file, tied together. When there is no snow, or not enough, for sledges, household belongings, food, tents, small children and old people are carried on pack animals, whose usual load is from 65 to 90lb (29–41kg). In snow the load is transferred to sledges, of which there are several types, depending on function (p 103). They carry much more than a pack animal, from 220 to 330lb (100–150kg), and the usual train is consequently smaller with six or seven animals. Those able to do so travel on skis and everything goes more smoothly – at least until the inevitable snags are met.

Modern developments

The classic reindeer nomadism described above is now largely a matter of history. What is dubiously termed the march of progress has steadily transformed it at a speed which the inflation of recent years has increased. Snow-scooter, cars, motor-boats, even helicopters, controlled by telephone and transceivers, are used to manage the reindeer and to carry the loads they formerly bore. The paid hand has taken over from the unpaid member of the family. Cabins have replaced tents at stages on the migration routes. The Lapps' grazing and calving grounds are threatened, or destroyed, by vast developments to provide raw materials, energy, or even holiday amusement, for other peoples. The economic, and thus the social, basis of the old life is under permanent attack. So are the Lapps' ancient rights, even by the Swedish State which, in 1976, won a legal case which confirmed its bitterly contested powers to continue its development policies on Lapp lands.

The difficulties reindeer breeders face may most tellingly be illustrated by specific examples, and the following account is based on unpublished material kindly made available to the author by the authorities in Norrbotten in the summer of 1975. The Karesuando district of the north Swedish county of Norrbotten has the largest concentration of Lapps in the country. In 1973, 383 households (1,290 individuals) in 193 groups owned 63,372 reindeer. However, 144 groups had less than 300 reindeer and only 15 over 500 – the minimum number then required to make ends meet. The average individual income from reindeer in 1972 was only 3,900 crowns. To raise it to subsistence level with the existing structure of reindeer management would then have required an annual subvention of 15 million crowns, and this was before the 'oil inflation'. Even assuming that demographic and social trends among the Lapps ensured its successful application, such a sum could not be found.

In fact this should not be assumed. Over 85 per cent of Norrbotten's inhabitants live within twenty miles of the main centres of population. Most Lapps now have permanent homes which require a steady cash outlay to maintain. Reindeer do not provide this. However attractive in terms of 'job satisfaction' reindeer-management on present lines may be, it undoubtedly involves a great deal of disguised unemployment in terms of a full year's work. To provide an adequate income, alternative or supplementary work is needed. Hence the importance of the various development schemes, of subsidised handicrafts, and of tourism. Reindeer breeding itself will have to become more rationalised with local concentrations of larger herds employing fewer men. Otherwise – and it's difficult to reject the claim – in the words of the Governor of Norrbotten, 'mountain life in Lapland will be on the brink of catastrophe'.

The experience of a major group of Skolt Lapps north of Lake Inari provides a comparable illustration of drastic change, described in Pertti J. Pelto's *The Snowmobile Revolution*. From being a remote, self-sufficient unit with stable, traditional values and a cohesive, egalitarian society,

16 Rounding up reindeer (*Teuvo Kanerva*)

They have become a divided society, impoverished as a group, because their dependence on cash, external sources of energy and a more capital-intensive economy has grown since the 1960s, when the introduction of the first effective small snowmobile, the Canadian 'skidoo', revolutionised reindeer-herding and transport. The richer members of the community, who alone could afford these machines, have become richer, earlier smaller and acceptable differentiations being thus uncomfortably accentuated. The young, more mechanically minded than the old, have gained status, and money, to the detriment of their elders, whose traditional skills are now irrelevant and whose authority is consequently undermined. Furthermore, the intimate association with a sensitive and responsive animal, which was at the heart of the old system of reindeer-herding, has been replaced by occasional mechanised round-ups, impersonal and frightening. The reindeer, now left on their own for most of the year, have become half-wild. Their fertility has dropped noticeably. Their usefulness as draught animals has become negligible. The enjoyable and sociable freight trip to Norway, which took three days and required much time and effort to prepare and to carry out, is now made in a few hours by a couple of men with a snowmobile. The satisfying old life has been destroyed.

About 15 per cent of all Lapps live from reindeer-breeding, reindeer nomads, mainly in Sweden, comprising about 10 per cent of the total. The administrative machinery to handle their affairs has recently developed on generally similar lines in Finland, Norway and Sweden. All three countries divide the reindeer areas into various districts with Lapps participating in their management. They also have a tripartite committee for dealing with problems of joint interest – migration across frontiers, poaching, pest control and so on. But there are several important differences. In particular, in the reindeer territory of Finland—most of the County of Lapland and the northern parts of Uleåborg County—all Finnish citizens resident there, not only Lapps, are entitled to own reindeer. Of the 58 reindeer districts in this region only 12 are in the Lapp communes (Enontekiö, Inari, Sodankylä and Utsjoki), which contain 90 per cent out of all Finish Lapps. Of a national total of some 200,000 reindeer, the Lapps own only about a third, and about a third of all Finnish Lapps are primarily reindeer-breeders. Since 1948 there has been a Central Federation of Reindeer Breeders' Associations, which has fostered co-operation in management and marketing. Membership of an association is compulsory. In Norway similarly both Lapps and Norwegians breed reindeer, but in separate regions. Broadly speaking, the northern counties down to the Rorøs district are reserved for Lapps. There is a National Association of Lapp Reindeer Breeders, who now number about 1,800 with 180,000 or so animals. There are also estimated to be about 50,000 wild reindeer in Norway.

In Sweden by contrast, only Lapps may own reindeer, a right reiterated in the latest Reindeer Management Law of 1971, which also lays down detailed provisions on organisation, seasonal grazing grounds and so on, for both Mountain and Forest Lapps. The influential National Association of Swedish Lapps looks after reindeer-breeders' interests at the national level, special sections, in which Lapps work, in each agricultural department of the northern counties at the local level. There are at present nearly 200,000 reindeer in Sweden. Numbers fell in the early 1970s to about 120,000 from an annual average of about 175,000, due to successive bad winters and over-grazing: the reindeer-lichen is a weak link here, since it takes about twenty years to regenerate. In the last two seasons, however, the herds, particularly those of the Mountain Lapps, have increased; in Norrbotten alone in 1976 there were about 140,000. Official figures in any case are generally considered too low, since it is on them that taxes are paid, and there is thus an inducement to minimise them.

Against the above background of decline and drastic change it is worth recording that the Lapps are determined to maintain their close association with the reindeer. They see it as the cardinal element in their cultural heritage. An opinion poll in 1976 among Lapp women, whose move to more comfortable permanent homes is so often adduced as a major reason for the decline of nomadic herding, showed that over half, including the younger ones, considered that reindeer-breeding had a future. A little earlier a Lapp conference recorded its view that without reindeer there could be no true Lapp culture. But what future harsh economic pressures will allow remains to be seen.

4

TRADITIONAL SOCIETY

Beneath the material trappings of an increasingly uniform and urban Western civilisation the Lapps still retain certain basic elements of their traditional society. The extent and the particular manifestations of this vary from group to group, but the old sense of community and family ties remain generally strong. In this, as in other respects, the Mountain and the Skolt Lapps are the chief guardians of tradition. Among the older generation the old attitude to important family events such as marriage, and conformity with ancient customs, taboos even, such as the cooking of meat by men, not women, are fairly widespread. In organisational terms Lapp society was, and in some groups still is, based on the communal activity of the *siida*, mentioned earlier in connection with the reindeer management of the Mountain Lapps. It has inevitably moulded their whole social psychology.

The siida

The *siida* is a group of a few families and of up to about ninety persons co-operating together either to hunt and fish or to manage their reindeer. The concept is found throughout Lapland, as is the name in over twenty variants. Its origins and ramifications have been the subject of considerable research and discussion. It is old: the 'Lapp villages' mentioned in official papers from the sixteenth century were identical with already established *siida*. The first time many places in north Scandinavia are mentioned they are described, in the appropriate local dialect, as *siida* – Laissita, for example. The system most probably dates from the stage of large-scale reindeer-hunting before the development of reindeer nomadism. Such activity had to be a communal effort with an accepted leader to organise it. He tended to come from a dominant family and, originally, probably also had religious functions. Equally, if all participate in productive activity, all are entitled to their due share of its results. Hence the *siida* looked after all its members and fostered an admirable communal solidarity. Externally it protected its own interests and territory against outsiders.

Within this general framework the system is flexible in response to local and seasonal requirements: at certain times of the year, for example, the Mountain Lapp *siida* splits into smaller groups for specific purposes, combining again for major co-operative efforts, such as the autumn round-up. Similarly, although tended jointly on communal grazing-grounds, reindeer are owned privately. In organisational terms, the Skolt Lapps have developed the concept further to a more formal self-governing community with a council of elders (*norrāz*), composed of heads of families, and an elected headman with a deputy. The council supervises the management of the group's reindeer and land, on which each family is allotted an area for its own use for fishing, hunting, firewood and so on; has a judicial role in settling disputes; and was formerly responsible for paying taxes for the whole *sijd* (as the Skolts call it).

In Norway and Sweden the system was more autocratic with the headman (*siida-ised*) exercising sole authority. This facilitated the integration of the Lapps into the new administrative machinery since this leader was simply made responsible to the central government as well as to his own people. In its actual workings the old Lapp social system must have been more complex than the above brief account indicates. But the Lapps' way of life precluded any larger political organisation; and there has never been a Lapp state. Nor, despite accounts in sagas and early histories, have there ever been Lapp kings in the true sense. Such references to them are now taken to reflect the strong local position of powerful outsiders, such as Ottar or the Birkarls.

Kinship and customs

Relationships between the different members of the traditional Lapp society were regulated by a complicated kinship system, of which many traces remain. Age was its chief determinant: Lappish has a large and precise terminology to describe various members of different generations. There are, for example, three grades of cousin, each with its own name. On the other hand – probably reflecting the rules governing permitted marriages between kinsfolk – the same names are used for certain of both the father's and the mother's close relations, such as their brothers and sisters and first cousins. The complexities of the full system are not wholly understood and provide a fascinating field of research for social anthropologists.

Courtship ceremonials retained much of their ancient flavour until recently; those of marriage less so. There were, of course, local variations. In Finnmark, for example, if a girl allowed her suitor to pull a mitten off her hand, this indicated her approval of his suit. Generally the formal proposal was a big affair with the suitor coming to the girl's abode with a large party, the key member of which was the 'head of the wooing', a man, or occasionally a woman, of some standing, to arrange the whole business according to accepted rules. The girl's parents, for example, would play down the character and abilities of the suitor as presented by his champion and make out that their daughter was a pearl beyond price. The whole charade indeed was played out to settle the dowry as much as to agree on the marriage. The young people meanwhile, whether praised or disparaged, were expected to keep quiet and to pretend the discussion was no concern of theirs. The wooing party had to provide refreshments including ample supplies of brandy and presents for the girl's family on each visit: cynics said that courtship was occasionally deliberately protracted by the bride's family to maintain such largesse. There is certainly a Finnish proverb that one does not win a wife in Lapland without spirits. The betrothal in early days was signalled by an ancient, and rather charming, custom mentioned by Olaus Magnus and others. 'In the presence of friends and blood relations', he says, 'the parents ratify their children's marriage bond through fire, which is done by showering fire over them from steel and flint.' The idea was that, just as this hidden fire became visible in sparks, so should the hidden fire of their love produce children.

The bride's parents produced the dowry – basic household goods with some larger object of value, a reindeer among the Mountain Lapps; a reindeer, a fishing-net or a sledge among the Skolts; a cow, a few sheep or a plot of land among the settled Lapps. The young husband customarily lived with, and worked for, his wife's family for a year after the marriage. This, almost certainly wrongly, has led to conjectures that Lapp society was originally matriarchal. But these old customs do reflect primitive forms of marriage, such as the buying or abducting of wives, well known from the Ancient World and still practised by many peoples.

The marriage ceremony itself has long been a Church affair, generally Lutheran but, among the Skolts, in accordance with the more complicated Russian Orthodox rites. Lapp weddings are still a dazzling affair, with everybody in their colourful best costume, and the women shining with silver and gold. Earlier there was considerable symbolism – the bride letting down her coiffed hair, for example, and presenting the hairband to her closest unmarried female relative, much as English brides give their bouquets to their closest friends. The bride's parents provide the marriage feast.

Names are for various magic reasons of great significance to primitive people. Hence the old Lapps took great care to give their children the right name according to their customs. This was usually that of someone who had died recently and, if the new child died, the name was given to the next infant to be born of the same sex. As Christianity spread, the Church, for its own good reasons, long forbade the use of the old names such as Juksa, Motle or Sarre. A few survived, however, as first names – Sabba and Sarak, for example, not uncommon today. They were kept in use by the widespread Lapp custom at the period of transition to Christianity of holding a second surreptitious baptism on return from church to 'wash away' the Christian name and replace it with a 'stronger' old one.

Further changes were caused by the insistence of the new bureaucracy that Lapps, like other citizens, should register with surnames. These they produced in several ways. The equivalent of 'son' or 'daughter' would be added to the father's or mother's name – Aslaksen or Nilsdotter for example. Or the name of a parent was simply placed second, as in Turi or Guttorm. Or the names of places or unusual occupations (often in the Scandinavian form) would be used as surnames. Nicknames and diminutives, common among the Lapps as among other closely knit communities, were also employed. Concurrently standard Christian names, in either Scandinavian or Lappish version, came into use – Anders (Anta, Anti), Sigrid (Sigga). Among the Mountain Lapps in particular

17 Lapp woman, carrying her baby in a traditional cradle (*Nordiska Museet, Stockholm*)

women commonly retained their old surname after marriage. Recently of course ordinary Scandinavian names have been used, although in the last few years a tendency to return to Lappish names may be discerned, reflecting the new trend to assert a Lapp identity.

It is highly probable that in olden times the Lapps ended, with their consent, the lives of those who had become too old and infirm to accompany them on their migrations. One method was to push them over a precipice on a sledge – 'the blessed journey'; another was to drop them through a hole in the ice of a frozen lake. Such an end, among their own people and their beloved mountains and lakes, certainly accords with the nomad psychology. The author has been told of aged Lapps who, a generation or so ago, slipped out of camp in extreme weather to be found dead a short distance away. The Lapps now have old people's homes, from which it must be said many have chosen to return to the freedom of the wilds. Or the old folk can see out their days in comfortable houses at winter quarters. In this, as in other less final matters, the Lapps now increasingly conform with general practice.

With modern communications a Lapp who dies in the mountains will be brought to a mortuary within a few hours. Previously he would have been buried, either permanently or temporarily, near where he died, a special opening having been made in the tent wall to avoid the corpse leaving by the front door. Originally the body was put in a cave or under a cairn or between two trees beneath pieces of wood. From the early seventeenth century, however, burials began to be concentrated in specific places, particularly on certain islands, although high in the summer grazing-grounds simple crosses still stand to mark a solitary grave. It was long the custom to place in the crude wooden coffin or birch-bark shroud, objects of use to the departed in the next world – an axe, a tinder-box, a knife, a pipe and food. A ring of the Lapps' sacred metal, brass, also used to be placed on the arm, an ancient and widespread practice. Similarly, the reindeer which had pulled him to the cemetery, was slaughtered after three days. For most of the year the ground was too hard to permit interment, but the cold did allow the body to be moved to the churchyard, if so desired, for subsequent burial when the thaw softened the ground sufficiently for a grave to be dug.

18 Jokkmokk old church, showing compartments in the thickness of the fence to store bodies in cold weather

Hence old Lapp churches such as Jokkmokk have special outdoor compartments for storing bodies.

The apparently favoured position of the youngest son is the most distinctive feature of traditional Lapp rules of inheritance. He invariably inherited his father's reindeer. Among the Skolts and in parts of Finnmark he also inherited, and usually still does, the home and contents and the rights to family land. The underlying concept is that, as youngest son, he is unlikely to have had the time and opportunity to make his way in the world like his elder brothers, who are presumed to have gained both wife and portion by the time of the father's death. Among eastern Lapps, moreover, the youngest son was expected to stay at home to care for his aging parents. The inheritance was therefore due recompense, but it also involved a continued responsibility for looking after his mother and any unmarried sisters.

One other facet of the old ways may briefly be mentioned. This is the

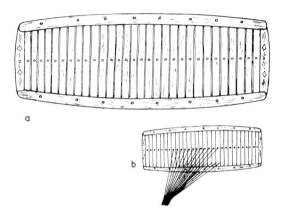

19 Ribbon-weaving reed made of reindeer bone: a) shows the holes and slats; b) the threads in position

clear division between men's work and women's work. The reasons are partly practical, partly superstitious; the primitive and widespread attitude to female functions playing a major role. Although ancient accounts speak of men and women hunting together, hunting has been an exclusively male pursuit since adequate records began. Men also prepare and cook meat, although this may be done by women when on a journey or if no men are present. Formerly the men made boats – Lapp sewn-boats were famous – sledges and the various panniers, saddles and travelling accoutrements. They still make utensils and implements of wood and bone. Women are traditionally responsible for making clothes and accessories, gloves, boots, belts and so on, and for preparing the appropriate material – dressing skins, spinning and dyeing wool, drawing pewter-thread. Both men and women produced beaten silver ornaments for belts or traditional necklaces. The aesthetic aspects of these handicrafts are dealt with in Chapter 7.

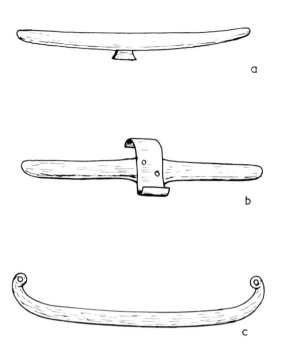

20 Implements in wood and metal: a) and b) skin-scrapers; c) shammy iron

Hunting

The Lapps have been renowned as hunters from earliest times, their ability to overtake their quarry on skis in winter adding to their fame. They have always been excellent marksmen, whether with bow or gun. Traditionally, their most important quarry was the bear; but a bear-hunt with all its ceremonies was essentially a religious ritual (p98). The reindeer and the beaver were the animals most hunted in the normal sense. As noted earlier, the reindeer had to be saved from extinction by a radical change in the Lapps' attitude to it. The beaver, because its skin was used to pay taxes, was virtually exterminated and has not been hunted for many years. The advent of, and subsequent improvements to, the gun were chiefly responsible for these changes, as they were for the decline of many ingenious old methods of hunting and trapping. Some, however, are still in use, since they are both economical and effective. Others are worth mentioning to illustrate this aspect of traditional life.

Several general considerations apply to all Lapp hunting. There is the dramatic difference between summer and winter: it is in winter that the pelts of fur-bearing animals are at their best. There is the importance of well-trained dogs. Earlier there was the excellence of the Lapps' indigenous equipment: skis have been mentioned. The Lapp bow was also unusually effective. Unlike other western European bows it was laminated like the Tartar compound bow. It was made of two strips of wood, usually pine and sallow, sometimes birch, glued together with a special fish glue made of perch skins, and bound along the whole length with narrow strips of birch bark. It was about 6ft (1.8m) long, 1in (2.5cm) or more thick and from 1½ to 1in (4–2.5cm) wide, tapering towards the ends. There was a ferrule and a 'basket' on the bottom end to enable it to be used as a ski-stick. Different arrow-heads were used for different targets. They were made of bone, iron, or the beak of a diver. Forked tips were often used for birds, blunt tips for fur-bearing animals to avoid undue damage to their skins. It was also said that, to the same end, the expert Lapps would often shoot an animal through its muzzle. For smaller game a crossbow with bolts was often used. A hunter on skis would carry his bow in his left hand as a staff, his quiver on his back and a spear (also with basket and spike at the bottom) in his right hand. The ordinary spear was over 6ft (1.8m) long, the bear spear not much longer but much stouter, with a head about a foot long and the top part of the staff of metal to prevent the bear biting it off. The spear sometimes had a bone snow-shovel at the bottom instead of a basket (Illus. 21). Lapp hunters and fishermen had many taboos, some of which remain in discreet use, as in many other countries. There were lucky and unlucky days. Women should not cross their path as they were setting out, for which reason they used to go out through the 'sacred back door' of the tent which women were never permitted to use.

Beavers used to be hunted – 'fished' was the old term – by the whole *siida* in early winter when streams and lakes were frozen, but not too thickly. A favourite method was to build an obstruction of poles up to

73

the surface of the water, around, but several feet away from, the beaver's lodge, and touching the bank on both sides of it. It led into a dead-end, which was closed by a trap-door falling down when the animal pushed, or bit through, the osier retaining it, one end of which was among a bait of pieces of aspen bark, of which the beaver is inordinately fond. Another method was to use a sort of large lobster-pot weighted down with stones and again baited with aspen bark. If the animal did not extricate itself within an hour or so – the maximum time it can stay under water – it drowned. However, in the charming words of a seventeenth century account, 'it not infrequently happens that, if there are two beavers, man and wife, one helps the other to open the door and provide a way out of the trap'. Ordinary nets and spring-traps were also used.

The hated wolf was hunted by one man on skis, with a stout staff and a knife as his only weapons: a gun was too cumbersome. The beast was chased, sometimes for many hours, until it was too tired to go any further and turned at bay. The hunter would then hit it hard on the muzzle or base of the spine to incapacitate it. The wolf would try to bite the staff and, while he was thus engaged, the hunter stabbed him. There are old Lapps still alive who hunted wolves professionally in this way, as Johan Turi did. One of his tips is that, if the wolf gets hold of one's hand, one must never try to pull it away. Instead one should push it right down the wolf's throat, squeeze his windpipe to make him keep his jaws open, and knife him with the free hand! Today's intrepid hunters now shoot wolves from helicopters with repeating rifles (though this is illegal in Sweden). Poison and traps – both traditional heavy break-backs of wood and strong metal spring-traps – are also used in the battle against the wolf.

The wolverines' own gluttonous habits were exploited to catch them. These beasts like to gorge themselves so uncomfortably full that they find it necessary to void their guts by squeezing themselves between two trees close together. Traps would be set in such places. They were also flushed from their lairs by smoke or dogs, as martens often were. The wily fox is caught by the comparable cunning of man. Fox-poles, about 6ft (1.8m) high, with one or two sharp-edged, deep, notches are erected in promising places with an attractive bait on top (Illus. 22). When the

21   Bear spear with reindeer-horn snow shovel   22   Fox trap

fox jumps to get at the bait there is a good chance that his paw will catch in the notch and he will be caught, dangling helplessly. A poisonous lichen (*Letharia vulpina*, 'wolf-moss') was also sometimes mixed with a juicy bait.

Small furred animals were hunted in various ways calculated to do least damage to their pelts. Stoats were trapped in miniature versions of fox-poles and pitfalls or cage-traps, or shot with blunt arrows. So were squirrels which, in the forest trees, were also killed by long switches with pointed iron tips. Spring-traps were placed in shallow water at suitable places to take otters, which were also hunted by men and dogs, the animal's escape being made more difficult by damming streams and erecting obstacles on the banks. Innumerable seals have been harpooned from earliest times, and elk shot. The hunter benefits from the propensity of elks to return to their fallen comrades to see what has happened, and can often bag several in one place.

Ptarmigans, capercaillies, geese, swans and, near the sea, puffins and auks are taken for food. They are both shot and trapped. Ptarmigans are enticed into an area sewn with snares by a trail of birch buds, capercailzies into conical shelters on sandy ground near the roots of a fallen tree, a favourite resting-place. Water-birds are caught in spring-traps among the weeds they forage in. Puffins and other edible sea-birds are netted or caught in nooses on long poles. Some old accounts credit the Sea Lapps with the ability to summon auks within range of a club by magic songs.

Fishing

Apart from enormous catches of sea-fish off the Arctic Coast the Lapps have long reaped a rich harvest, especially of salmon, whitefish and pike, from the rivers and lakes of their land. From the seventeenth century netting has been the most productive method, using both set (gill) nets and seines (curved nets with a strong 'purse' at their outer point and long 'wings' which are pulled in to the shore along the bottom). Set nets are usually about 120ft (36m) long, seines up to 600ft (183m) in length. Traditional nets have their top edges strengthened with pine roots. Their floats are of birch bark, or pine wood for the bigger seines, their sinkers of stone wrapped in birch bark. The net itself is made of home-spun hemp line with small or large meshes from about ½in (1.3cm) wide to 'a hand's breadth plus a thumb's breadth' (for salmon), depending on its role. It is camouflaged by a dye made of birch root, brown fungi and wood-ash. Draw ropes are of roots, lighter and more resistant to water than hemp. The ubiquitous and indestructible nylon, however, is replacing the old equipment, with empty plastic containers as floats. Set nets are used from the time the ice breaks up to June and from early August to the beginning of winter, seines in the summer. But both have long been occasionally used through the ice.

Other methods include fish spearing, often at night with the aid of flares and especially for salmon; but this is now illegal. Floating nets and traps of stakes in specified stretches of the rivers, which families inherit, are the main methods of catching salmon today. Fishing is strictly controlled in the interests of conserving the stock: on the Tana and Utsjoki rivers, for example, nets must be taken in on Saturdays and Sundays to allow the fish to run. In small streams little dams and traps of birch twigs are built to catch trout and grayling. In the cold season burbot are taken on lines, traditionally of pine roots with hooks of tough juniper wood. They have also been caught for hundreds of years, when the ice is transparent, by banging the ice above them with a heavy stick and stunning them. Lines are dropped for whitefish through holes in the ice of frozen lakes in winter, the fishermen erecting a shelter above the hole both to prevent it freezing and for their own convenience. Fly-fishing with a rod, introduced by the British in the middle of last century, is practised as a sport.

Food and drink

The traditional Lapp foods are reindeer products and fish with game, fowl, berries and wild herbs in season. Though often monotonous, the diet is highly nutrititious with much animal protein. Laestadius remarks in his *Lapland Journey*: 'Fresh fish and fowl with reindeer milk and berries are delicacies, not a meal to turn one's nose up at.' Little cereal would be eaten, and that as porridge, or as a constituent of sausages or blood gruel, as well as in unleavened, flat barley-bread baked on a hot flat stone, occasionally as 'pan-bread' made, as in the west of Ireland, in the bottom of a cauldron. The Skolts have long baked rye-bread in ovens and have drunk Russian tea, but no reindeer milk, unlike other Lapps who 'coffee-house' incessantly between meals, adding a pinch of salt to the coffee to bring out its flavour. Otherwise water is the usual drink; camps are sited near good water, though the fastidious Lapp will often use a drinking-tube at a spring. In winter a kettle of warm water is kept in the tent for drinking. Celebrations are marked by a considerable consumption of spirits: historically the Lapps have a not wholly justified reputation as brandy-drinkers dating from the days when foreign merchants plied them with drink at fairs to take advantage of them, or from observers' accounts of their seasonal jollifications. There are, of course, differences between the food eaten in summer and winter, also between that of different groups. All, however, have in recent years increasingly turned to the standard groceries, tinned milk, white bread, white sugar and convenient carbohydrates. But reindeer meat and fish are still important foods.

The Mountain Lapps are more reliant on the reindeer than other groups who can get more fish with meat and milk from cows, sheep and goats; poultry and eggs, and vegetables such as potatoes and turnips. Meat eaten hot is almost invariably boiled and lightly cooked. The broth is drunk, after most of the fat has been skimmed off for use as lard. The tongue of a reindeer, the tail and the marrow-bones, are great delicacies. These and the pieces most easily cooked are eaten first when a reindeer is slaughtered. Meat is traditionally shared out according to certain, undoubtedly ancient, rules about who gets which piece and in what order. The main, hot, meal is eaten late in the evening; cold and dry food – smoked meat and cheese – being consumed during the day, apart from a bowl of broth or porridge sometimes as the first thing in the morning. The Lapps, like other nomads, are traditionally heavy eaters, but can also go long periods without food.

Other mammals considered clean are also eaten – elk, squirrel and, formerly, beaver. Bear meat, especially the soles of the feet, was the supreme delicacy for the old Lapps. The Skolts, however, have never eaten it, not, as their neighbours maintain, because they often look as if they are descended from bears, but because no members of the Orthodox Church do. Seals, otters and martens have also provided food and, in hard times, even foxes and wolverines, but never wolves. Rather surprisingly the western Lapps at any rate are reluctant to eat hares. Squirrel stomachs are roasted whole and full of pine and spruce seeds by Finnish Lapps. Some of these unusual foods have in fact a high dietetic value and, almost instinctively, the Lapps seem aware of this. Their responses are remarkably sensitive. For example, there is a well-known story that, after buying the original margarine for a few years as a cheaper substitute for butter, they went back to butter on the grounds that margarine spoiled the sight. Until a later product, reinforced with vitamins after laborious researches had revealed earlier shortcomings, was put on sale, it probably did.

78

Fish is usually boiled fresh and often eaten cold. The liquor is drunk, not just thrown away. Fish and meat are sometimes cooked in the same pot. The most important edible fish are whitefish, bleak and grayling in lakes, Alpine char and salmon trout in mountain tarns and streams, salmon in the bigger rivers and off their mouths, cod species, flounders, halibut and haddock in the sea. Pike, perch and burbot are a second best. Apart from boiling, fish may be cooked by grilling on a spit in its own juices, the guts being left in; this is usual when the Lapp is on a journey. A lot of fish is dried by sun and air. The sometimes enormous frames for drying cod are a feature of the Arctic Coast, as are the carefully sited drying, or smoking, huts of the Fisher Lapps around Lake Inari. Many fish, especially salmon and whitefish, are salted; but too lightly for the taste of most outsiders who find it putrid rather than preserved. Fish is eaten in many other ways. Dried fish has for centuries been pulverised to make a 'fish-bread', dried roe is mixed with flour. Fish is boiled, boned, and pounded in a mortar with berries and eaten cold. It is also often eaten raw.

Other items, common or merely quaint, of the traditional diet may be mentioned, above all the abundant, unusually big, berries of Lapland – cloudberries, crowberries, bilberries. They are eaten both fresh and preserved. Cloudberries are simmered in their own juice, sprinkled with salt and buried in birch-bark containers for future use. Herbs, such as angelica or sorrel, add flavour and essential anti-scorbutics to the diet. Young stalks of angelica are eaten raw, roasted, or cooked in whey and stored in a cleaned reindeer stomach for winter use. Wild onions (*Allium spp.*) are used as flavouring, as is upland scurvy grass (*Cochlearia alpina*). Various edible fungi are consumed in the autumn. Eggs of larger birds such as gulls, ducks and mergansers, are taken from their natural nests or artificial nesting-boxes, and provide a welcome addition to the Lapp table. In hard times, or from taste, the juicy inner bark of the pine (*Pinus silvestris*) is shredded and eaten in various forms, including the famous 'bark bread'. Both men and older women have smoked pipes since the introduction of tobacco.

Health and medicine

The good health of the Lapps is famous. In the seventeenth century, Samuel Rheen, supporting other of Scheffer's sources, says: 'the Lapps are naturally a healthy people who are not generally afflicted with the infirmities of the body, as are the people of other nations.' They lived long and died of old age, not illness. They had neither doctors nor need of them, although, as becomes apparent below, they had many medicines of their own. The Lapps' fitness to some extent reflects the survival of the fittest in rigorous conditions, but it is also due to a healthy environment and a well-adjusted, though strenuous, life. Many travellers have extolled the invigorating effects of Lapland's pure air, bright sun and majestic vistas. 'Never in all my days have I felt fitter than now', Linnaeus remarked. Nearly 200 years later Frank Hedges Butler, in his *Through Lapland with Skis and Reindeer,* was similarly enthusiastic and expatiated on the region's tourist potential as a second Switzerland. The Lapps' traditional diet is also good, while the care a traditional society takes of its old is a major factor in their continued well-being.

Inflammation of the eyes caused by long exposure to smoke inside tents, sometimes by snow-glare, and frequently leading to blindness in old age, was the commonest ailment among Lapps until recently. Other afflictions were colds, dyspepsia, vertigo, pneumonia and 'aches and pains' in back and bones; but acute and chronic rheumatism were, somewhat surprisingly, rare, and virtually unknown among the nomads. Neuroses were fairly common, but mental illness rare. The main contagious disease was measles. Tuberculosis was not a scourge but, if established in a family, would run through it. Organic heart diseases, anaemia and diabetes were seldom encountered. In recent decades, however, an inferior diet richer in carbohydrates and different living conditions have contributed to a noticeable deterioration in the health of the Lapps, and they increasingly exhibit the more usual Western pattern of illness. The incidence of tooth decay and infantile rickets in particular has increased, while the attitudes of a modern materialistic society have aggravated the psychosomatic problems of old age.

Of the many Lapp remedies – the Norwegian author, Adolf Steen, has listed 166 *materia medica* for 125 ailments – the commonest was the counter-irritant one of moxibustion, of ancient Chinese origin. This consists in the application of heat, produced by burning certain substances, to the afflicted part. The substance generally used by the Lapps was thin strips of birch wood or, for sensitive areas such as swollen lips, a fungus (*Polyporus fomentarius*) which smouldered. Heat was employed on other occasions also, a poultice of slices of melting cheese being applied to frostbite. Backache was massaged with snake-fat, if the widely carried charm of a beaver's tooth in the back of one's belt had not kept it away. Toothache was treated by jabbing the gum with a splinter until blood flowed. Reindeer blood was drunk to treat many conditions such as exhaustion, scurvy and puerperal fever; reindeer excrement was applied to swellings, burns, earache; and reindeer urine drunk for alcoholism, stomach-cramp and other troubles. The list is long, a curious mixture of superstition, revolting practices and shrewd treatment, with the sufferer's belief in the value of the remedy, as always, of cardinal importance. Fats and train-oil and the gall of various animals – bear, beaver, swan, raven – played an important role. Quicksilver and sulphur were also used, as were snails and the dried stomachs and skins of several animals.

There were many herbal remedies. Angelica, raw or boiled in milk, was the commonest. Chewed birch-bark and resin were kneaded into poultices. Parts of many plants were pressed into service – birch leaves, chickweed, coltsfoot, horsetail, juniper, absorbent mosses. A magic drum was often employed in diagnosis, and shamanistic powers in cures: there are accounts of shamans curing the patient but dying themselves. How much of this ancient medicine remains is difficult to say. All parts of Lapland now have modern health services. But many of the old remedies, as in remote districts elsewhere, are probably more often used than outsiders realise.

Pastimes

The gay and lively Lapps, when the rhythm of their life permits it, delight in talk and the social round. Such interests, and the hospitality shown to strangers, were formerly important in keeping in touch with the outside world and in educating the young. Fairs have served a similar purpose for hundreds of years at Arjeplog or Jokkmokk, for example, and formerly at Varanger (1571), Alta and Lyngen. They often coincided with church festivals and were the occasion for important family functions, which added to the general gaiety. Some favourite traditional themes of song and story are mentioned on page 125; they were extremely important in helping to pass the time enjoyably and usefully in the old society.

Before the advent of mechanical toys with functions limited by their very design, Lapp, and other, children had to make do with simpler, but often more imaginative, toys. These, like their games, normally imitated their elders' activities and were thus an initiation into adult life, whether in the care given to a crude doll or the rounding up of make-believe reindeer, a favourite game in which children carried antlers. Practice in lassoing, competitions in running, jumping, ski-ing and shooting were, and are, common pastimes. Adults, both men and women, vie with each other, in reindeer-racing, in long and high jumping and various team games. Some of these are very old. One, for example, resembles a trial of strength described in old Norse sagas. In it one contestant lies on his back with his legs in the air and his arms stretched out. The other stands on the hands of the prone player with his hands on his feet. The man on the ground throws the other as far as he can. Whoever throws furthest wins. There was another in which every man had a strong belt which his opponent gripped and, without any other holds, tried to force him to the ground. The Lapps are also fond of dancing: they used to favour distinctive jigs. The Skolts were once famous for their quadrilles.

The most distinctive indoor game is a board game called *tablo* (Illus. 23). There are several versions, such as 'wolf' *tablo*, or 'fox' *tablo*, the part of the animal being taken by one player, whom his opponent must corner before the beast 'eats' all his pieces. The counters may be either shaped pieces or just coffee-beans or bits of wood or bone. Moves are made according to set rules. In another version (*sakko*), moves depend on the throw of a dice. Card games have long been popular and among the young, various games which bring them together with an element, or chance, of romance – 'forfeits', guessing games, blind-man's buff. In their present more settled and urban environment the Lapps, like others, tend to pass the time in the usual pursuits of watching television or films, or in hobbies such as handicrafts; but most still go off regularly to the wilds to fish, to ski and to commune with nature as their ancestors did.

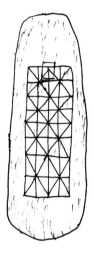

23 Tablo board

5

TRADITIONAL BELIEFS

The old Lapp religion was the animism typical of primitive peoples, with the special features of shamanism and the bear-cult common among Arctic races. Everything had a soul and power over men's lives. The great forces of nature, such as the sun, the winds, fertility and sickness, were the chief gods, but lesser spirits also had to be heeded and propitiated. The dead lived on in a better, shadow, world. The attitude of these powers was shown in signs and omens. More direct personal contact with the spirit world was achieved through magic drumming or the journey the shamanistic medium (*noaide*) made thither in a trance. It is thus not surprising that the Lapps were famous sorcerers, credited with the power of foreseeing the future and of controlling natural forces: for example, Christian IV's belief that they raised storms against him has been mentioned (p 35). This reputation still persists, particularly in relation to what is known in the Scottish Highlands as 'second sight' and to the ability to work minor miracles, such as the staunching of blood.

Beliefs and rituals, nevertheless, varied considerably. The western Lapps had a well developed cosmogony, with many similarities to that of the Norsemen. The Finnish Lapps, on the other hand, long maintained simpler concepts; their chief gods were thunder and local deities. Although there is, at least for Norway and Sweden, a wealth of information on the old religion, its formulation, in the light of modern anthropological research and theory, is considered too categorical and too simple. It consists largely of ecclesiastical and official accounts, including reports of prosecutions for heathen practices. In such circum-

24 and 25 Two *seide*: (*above*) Svaipa/Arjeplog (height 30in); (*below*) Pålnovuoddo/Jukkasjärvi (height 12in)

stances it is not surprising that the Lapps, under pressure sometimes to the point of death, suppressed or distorted certain matters. Conversely, the priests fitted what they learnt into the framework of their own beliefs and knowledge. Thus the similarities between many Lapp gods and those of the Norse pantheon were attributed to their acceptance by the Lapps from the Norwegians. Rafael Karsten's comment in his *The Religion of the Samek* is typical of the modern approach. He says 'the Scandinavian elements in the Lapps' religion belong rather to the periphery than to the nucleus. That a primitive people should 'borrow' virtually all its religion from some other people of a higher culture is a patent absurdity'. Some indeed now maintain that the Norwegians borrowed from the Lapps and the view is increasingly held that the old Lapp religion was of eastern origin. There is, however, general agreement that its oldest form was the worship of local idols on special cult sites and of a few dominant natural forces.

Cult sites and idols

The Lapps worshipped at a sacrificial site (*seide*), which was either public and used by the whole group, or private such as a sanctum in the home or, occasionally, a secret place out of doors. There must have been thousands. More than 800 have been recorded throughout Lapland, as well as traditions concerning several hundred more. They are exhaustively treated in Manker's splendid *Lapparnas Heliga Ställen* (The Lapps' Sacred Sites) which has an English summary. There are over 500 in Sweden. The various names by which they were known – *seide (seite, saita* etc), *saivo (saiva), passe (basse)*, for example – abound on the map as components of placenames. Such sites are usually distinguished by a curious, or awe-inspiring, feature. Many of them indeed are striking natural features – a mountain peak, a great gorge, a rock weathered into some odd shape, a 'double-bottomed' lake (a lake with a spring in its bottom). Elsewhere trees, sometimes crudely shaped into a human face and form, prominent rocks near a lake rich in fish, or waterfalls, constituted the site, and probably also the object, of veneration.

The manner of worship is well-known from old accounts and illustrations (Illus. 26). A small idol, whether a stone or, for the higher gods, a platform, would, like the typical pole-store, be placed on or surrounded by a bed of twigs. A semi-circle of antlers, occasionally of birch-branches, enclosed the 'altar', which the worshipper approached bareheaded, on his knees with his hands palm uppermost in supplication. On important occasions a priest officiated. More casually, fish heads or blood and entrails were deposited at, or smeared on, the sacred rock near a lake. Crude wooden idols, too, were erected: more frequently, as is now thought, than earlier believed. There is also evidence of a phallic cult. From the Middle Ages the Lapps, rather curiously, took to using a Swedish name *storjunkare*, 'grand squire', for their local gods.

Sacrifices were in the nature of a bargain, as well as a thank-offering; there are reports of a *seide* being knocked over for failing to keep its side of the bargain. The offerings varied enormously and may have included humans. The Norwegian school-teacher, Isaac Olsen, who listed 112

26   Ancient Lapp altar (seide) (Scheffer, Bodleian Library)

sacrificial sites in Varanger early in the eighteenth century, talks of
'. . . human bones and large blood sacrifices of both humans and animals'. An account of the Kemi Lapps in Finland a little earlier remarks *en
passant* that babies were no longer sacrificed; and there are more recent
traditions of this practice from north Sweden. The reindeer, or parts of it
especially the genitalia, was frequently offered up; but other animals,
dogs, cats, and fishes were also sacrificed. Spear-heads or arrow-heads
were deposited on the sacred site, as were valuable and significant trin-
kets. The *seide* of the eastern Lapps indeed appears sometimes to have
been adorned with gold and jewels. The magic drum was used in divination to discover the most propitious offerings. These might have to be
obtained from far away. Some Lapps from Jokkmokk, for example,
arraigned for heathen practices in 1687, had been over the mountains to
the Norwegian coast to get their prescribed victims. The main seasons
for important sacrifices were autumn and spring.

The family shrine (*boaššo*) was a space set apart at the back of the tent,
forbidden to women and entered by a separate entrance, the 'sacred back
door'. Here the head of the house kept his household god, his magic
drum and his weapons, and from here he offered family prayers and sacrifices. A minor goddess of hunting had her abode beneath this shrine.

Gods and priests

On a different plane from pure animism the Lapps worshipped many
gods personifying natural forces great and small, in the heavens, on earth
and below ground. The most important were two celestial deities with
extensive, but ill-defined, powers – Jubmel or Ibmel, and Radien-attje.
Jubmel, whose name and cult in various forms are found among most
Ural-Altaic peoples, was the original supreme god and represented the
power of the heavens, 'the day spring'. For Swedish Lapps, Radien-
attje, 'the ruling father', 'the great father', was more important. Elsewhere his attributes and functions largely merged with those of Varal-
den-olmai, 'the world man', the god of fertility and increase. With his
son, Radien-kiedde, and wife, Radien-akka, as Manker and Vorren
observe in their valuable *Lapp Life and Customs*, he formed 'a patriarchal

trio strangely reminiscent of the Christian Trinity'. He was also sometimes given a daughter, Radien-nieidda or Rana-neida, goddess of new
spring growth and greenery, the counterpart of the Norse Frøya. Similarly, the eastern Lapps' great god Tiermes, lord of thunder and
weather, was at one time held to be of Norse origin. His other, later,
name, Horagalles, is a direct translation of Thor's Old Norse name
'thunder man'. But Tiermes, like Jubmel, both as a concept and also
under many cognate names, is widely established among Arctic, and
other, peoples. Peive, the sun, was worshipped, as were Biegg-Olmai,
'wind man', and Tjas-olmai, 'blood man'. The night sky also held its
deities and is now thought to have played a more important role in the old
religion than earlier accounts indicate. Aske, later Mano, the moon,
ruled here. Major constellations were probably worshipped as well.

On earth there were many lesser gods. Maderakka, 'woman creator',
'earth mother', obtained souls from Radien-kiedde, converted them in
her womb to human seed and gave them to one of her three daughters,
Sarakka, 'spinning woman', to implant in the mortal mother. Sarakka
lived under the hearth and her role was to help at childbirth and rein-
deer-calving, spinning sinew thread when not thus employed. The
other daughters were Juks-akka, 'bow woman', who watched over
male children and could change a female into a male child in the womb
and whose symbol was a bow, and Uks-akka, who had the more
straightforward job of guarding the door. Other minor gods of earth included three Ailekes, 'men of the holy days', who saw to it that religious
festivals were duly observed.

At a lower supernatural level there were fairies and elves; there are
reports of sightings up to a generation or so ago. Elves, as often elsewhere, were always trying to substitute a changeling for a new-born
child. Hence the heathen baptism included the presentation to the infant
of an amulet, usually a miniature bow, to keep them away. One of the
many standard questions put by missionaries to prospective Lapp con-
verts asked whether they still had their 'bow'. Somewhat ironically, in
view of the fulminations of early churchmen against the Devil's work
among the Lapps, they had no such concept until the advent of Christianity. The power of Evil was seen as more specific. To some extent,

however, and after making due allowance for the confusing and multi-farious elements in his make-up, the cruel giant, Stallo, takes his place as an evil creature, but without the Devil's supernatural powers.

Below the ground lived the dead, Rota, god of sickness and death – to whom a horse would be sacrificed and buried so that he could ride away on it underground carrying the illness far from the sufferer for whom the rite was performed – and the familiars of the *noaide*. The dead had a world of their own, Jabmi-aimo, World of the Dead, or Mubbe-aimo, Other World, part of which, Saivo, formed the Lapp Happy Hunting Grounds, or Paradise. Certain special places on earth were also acknowledged as Saivo and, as such, were the sites of sacrifice. This was the spirit world the sorcerer visited in his trance.

Laymen performed routine rites and uttered appropriate incantations. The head of the family banged away manfully on his drum but, for the best results, one went to the expert, the *noaide*. This man, or very occasionally, woman, had to pass a strict examination in sorcery which required, among other things, that he should demonstrate to a panel of established practitioners that he could make a successful journey to the spirit world. The *noaide* officiated at major religious ceremonies and, for a fee, could be consulted privately. Unlike most priests he did not wear special vestments apart from a magic belt and cap. The belt, which was sometimes worn across the chest (over the right and under the left shoulder, like the sash of an Order of Chivalry) was decorated with rings and amulets of brass – the Lapps' sacred metal – silver, iron, copper or bone, miniature knives, bear's teeth and other charms. The cap was usually of skin, the hair inside; one acquired in north Sweden in 1908 is lined with red material and is of wolf-skin, with a pair of goat's horns on top and various charms typical of well-known cult finds, as well as several old coins.

Through the rhythmic beating of his magic drum, often accompanied by a repetitive chant, the shaman worked himself into a trance; the process is well-known in modern Western sub-cultures. Some, like other mediums, could 'go off' without external stimulation. In this state the soul was freed of its corporeal shell and journeyed to the spirit world. Here the *noaide* had the help of 'companions' of all sorts – whales, bears, fishes, whatever he chose – to achieve his purpose. If necessary, he could transform himself into a 'companion' appropriate for the task. When rival *noaide* fought there were some remarkable and rapid changes, and the loser sometimes never came out of his trance.

Magic drums

These sorcerers, as well as laymen, also resorted to the Lapps' famous magic drums for divination. They developed the art further than other people with similar techniques. Accordingly the early missionaries destroyed these potent heathen symbols by the hundred. Only 71 complete ones and a few pieces are now left. The British Museum has 3, the Uni-

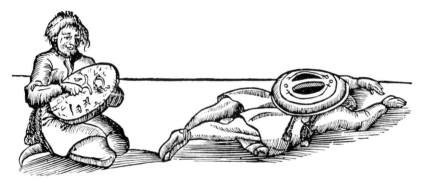

27   Playing a magic drum (*Scheffer, Bodleian Library*)

versity Museum of Cambridge 2 and there are many in Scandinavia, including a splendid collection of 29 in Nordiska Museet in Stockholm. A damaged one was acquired in north Norway as recently as 1925 and, in the last few years, replicas have been made by Lapp craftsmen in Sweden for museums and collectors. Although drums too big to move (and which were therefore burnt on the spot) are mentioned in seventeenth-century accounts of missionary activities in Finnish Lapland and there is a nineteenth-century reference to a copper drum in north Norway, those that remain are of manageable size and of wood. The magic drum is first mentioned in the *Chronicon Norvegicum* (c 1190), but

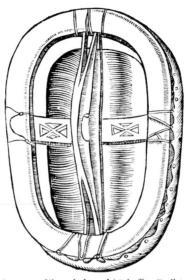

28 Back view of 'bowl-drum' (*Scheffer, Bodleian Library*)

was certainly in use much earlier.

The drums still extant (this account is based on Manker's exhaustive and magnificently produced *Die lappische Zaubertrommel, Acta Lapponica*, 1938, 1950). The Lapps' magic drums are all oval, or elliptical, in shape. Their size varies from 9in to 33½in (22.2–85cm) in height and 7in to 14in (17.8–35cm) in width. Their bodies are of pine or birch wood and are of two main types: 'bowl' drums (*kåbdes*) and 'sieve', or 'frame', drums (*gievre*). The 'bowl' type is hollowed out of a solid piece of wood and has oblong slots in its back to provide a hand-hold (Illus. 28). It is typical of northern Lapland. There are three sorts of frame drum: the curved frame, the ring frame and the angular frame (*kannus*). The curved-frame type is constructed of one thin strip of wood about 3in (8cm) deep, bent round to form a flat-sided drum. The ring type is made of a naturally curved piece of wood. These two types are found among southern Lapps. A few drums from Finland are made of two angular pieces of wood joined together to produce a suitable frame. Frame drums are kept in shape by a strut or struts across the back, which also provide a handle. The backs of 'bowl' drums and the sides and struts of frame drums are

Wind God (Bieggolmai)

Lapp tent

Beaver

Pole storage hut

Man on skis

Man hunting elk

29   Symbols from magic drums

30 Central motif of a magic drum from southern Lapland, showing the sign of the sun in the centre, with storm, wind, hunting, luck and others

usually richly carved with geometric designs. Charms of brass, silver and other metals, bone, teeth, miniature arrow- and spear-heads were attached to the drums, especially frame drums, by leather thongs wrapped with tin thread. Many southern drums have tin nails hammered into the frame; these are believed to record the number of bears killed through their use. A thong was attached to the bottom of the drum for fastening to its owner's belt when he was moving around.

The drum-skin, made of reindeer-calf skin, was secured to the body either by threads of sinew or rivets of bone or hard wood. It is always decorated with magic figures and symbols in red (the magic colour of blood). The pigment is chewed alder-bark, applied with a quill or pointed stick. Some drums have well over a hundred pictures and the whole subject forms an engrossing and complex study. Each picture – god, man, animal, building – is a self-contained concept which is of value in reading the message of the drum. There is no intention of recording incidents, or of telling a story. The higher gods, the common

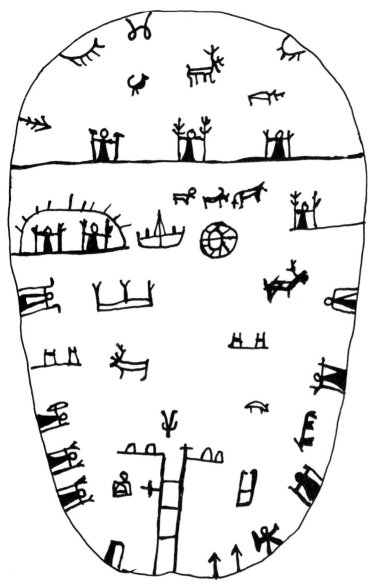

31 Magic drum, northern type, seventeenth-century or earlier, from Lule Lappuort

95

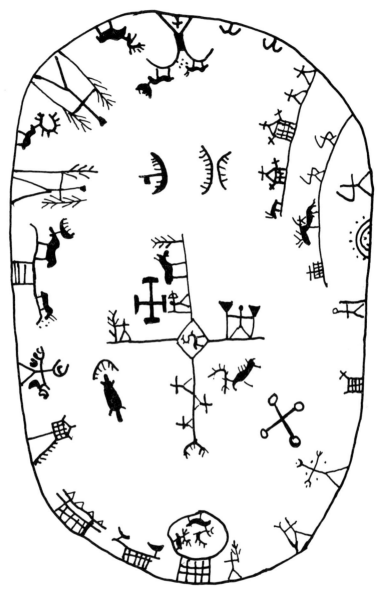

32   Seventeenth-century magic drum from southern Lapland

96

occupations of men, the more sought-after animals occur most frequently in standard symbols, sometimes so crude or so stylised as to be difficult to identify (Illus. 29). Southern drums give pride of place to the sun in the centre (Illus. 30).

There are regional differences in design. The pattern on northern drums is divided by parallel lines into different sections, each representing a different part of the Lapp universe. The sun, with or without rays, is placed in a top section (Illus. 31). His rays spread out to the four corners of the world, supporting other gods and other forms of life. Some drums combine southern and northern patterns: the top part is divided from the bottom by a horizontal line, while the rhomboid sun motif is placed in the centre of the lower section. A few drums, basically of southern type, have a spiral running through the pictures.

The method of operation was to put an indicator (*arpa, vuorbe*) – a triangular or circular bit of bone, a copper disc, a brass ring – on the skin and to tap the drum with a T-or Y-shaped hammer (*staura, vetjere*) as

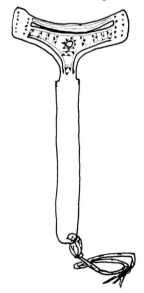

33   Hammer for magic drum from south/central Lapland. It is 17.1cm long and 8.6cm broad

shown in Illus. 33. This was usually of bone, although an iron one is known. It was decorated with mystic designs and the handle, with a thong at the bottom to attach it to the drum when not in use, was often covered with beaver-skin. As the drum-skin vibrated the indicator jumped – in early accounts it is called 'the frog', a magic animal – and moved across the surface. From its path and the symbols on which it settled, the sorcerer was able to make his prediction. In this, as in other religious and magic ceremonies, no woman was permitted to take part.

The bear cult

The bear has been much more to the Lapps, as to other Arctic peoples, than the biggest animal they hunt. Its size, strength and cunning have inspired respect and awe. Other qualities have endowed it with a special, in effect a sacred, status. It can walk on two feet like a man. It can climb trees. Its knowing look seems to reveal its wisdom even to the point of understanding human speech. It has the apparently supernatural ability of sleeping all winter. To the traditional Lapps it has been clearly a beast above all others and has been treated as such in all dealings. For example, its proper name in Lappish was never used in order to avoid the bear knowing it was being discussed. A special, oblique, 'bear language' was used by hunters. In it the bear was 'the grandfather of the hill', 'the sacred beast', or 'the woolly one'. For its parts and attributes old Norse names were used (since it was presumed to understand only Lappish). The hunting and disposal of the bear, to the Lapps as to other Northern peoples – especially in the days before firearms when the hunter was in close contact with his prey – accordingly developed into an elaborate magic ritual. The old bear festival died out in Lapland about a century ago; yet in the later evidence of lonely burials and the revelation of rituals unknown up to a few decades ago, it lingers on in folk memory. Many accounts present the general picture of it which is given below.

The first act in the drama begins with the discovery in the new snow of the winter den of the hibernating bear. The happy hunter first 'rings the bear' by walking three times round the spot at a distance of several hundred yards. He then returns to camp with the good news. He is hailed as a hero and gains the right to lead the hunt. Sacrifices are offered, the *noaide* consults his drum and, the omens being favourable, hunters and dogs set off. Our hero goes first, his stout bear-spear (Illus 21) adorned with a magic brass ring, the *noaide* next, and the boldest hunter, who will strike the first blow, third. The door of the bear's den is obstructed by placing poles across it to slow down his exit and improve the hunters' chance of spearing him. In Finland, at least, the first of many ritual songs was sung at this stage, asking the bear not to hurt the hunters. If this did not wake him, he was roused by other means and, when he came out, was killed. The hunters then sang another song which started by thanking the bear for not damaging their weapons. They then kicked the carcass with their skis in token of victory. The leading hunter tied a thin birch branch round its jaw, twisted the end thrice round his belt and jerked it repeatedly while singing another song, in which the others joined, shaking their spears. The bear might also be whipped with birch twigs. If it could not conveniently be taken back to camp the same day, it was covered with spruce branches and left until the next.

With or without the bear the hunters returned home, bursting into a triumphant song when within earshot of the camp. The women, now decked in jewels and finery, their faces covered with a piece of cloth, were waiting in the 'bear ringer's' tent. On hearing the hunters' song they replied with one of praise and welcome. Before the men entered the tent, our hero struck it three times with a willow wand with a brass ring on the end, uttering a ritual formula to announce the bear's death. He then entered the tent first, through the 'sacred' back door. The women cast aside their veils and put large brass rings before their faces through which they spat alder-bark juice on him, allowing the red liquid to stain their own faces and clothes. As the other hunters came in, they were similarly treated and their dogs too, if within range. The women then fastened a brass ring round the neck, one arm and one leg of each hunter with a piece of thread. The best food in the camp was then brought out, but the men left the women and both groups cooked and ate their meals separately. The men did not consort with their wives for the next three days, and the 'bear ringer' abstained for five.

And so the festival proceeded with many such complicated and significant rituals. The next stage was to bring the bear back on a sledge drawn by a reindeer: neither sledge nor reindeer could be used by a woman for a year. The men set up a separate tent decorated with brass rings and coils of shoe-grass. In it they skinned, prepared and cooked the bear. Great care was taken not to break its bones or damage its sinews or major arteries. Its muzzle was cut off and the man who had flayed it tied it to his face. The bear meat was not stored or preserved, but all consumed without salt in a great 3-day feast. The blood and fat were boiled first, the fat being carefully skimmed off into a brass cauldron. Blood was often smeared on tents, people and dogs. Special portions were given to the chief participants in the hunt in a prescribed order. The women ate separately, their food being carried to them by immature children. When all was eaten, the women again covered their faces, while the bones of the bear (its vertebrae threaded on a birch twig), head, genitalia and muzzle were taken away to be ceremonially buried. They were carefully assembled on a bed of twigs in proper order to assist its expected rebirth, and a birch-wood scoop full of chewed alder bark placed before the nose, its colour symbolising the red blood of life.

After the bear's burial its skin was stretched out on a frame or against a pile of snow. The women were blindfolded and given bows and arrows (sometimes alder twigs). They had to shoot, or throw, at the skin. If the first to hit it was married, it would be her husband who killed the next bear. If she was unmarried, she would be married within the year. She also had to sew a cross in pewter-thread for each of the hunters and the reindeer which pulled the bear home to wear round the neck for three days.

The festival concluded with purification ceremonies. The women scrubbed down the men. The men, in fresh clothes, then ran three times round the fireplace of their tent, holding on to the chains of the cauldron in which the bear meat had been cooked. The women meanwhile sang the last song and the 'bear ringer's' wife, with a pair of big gloves on her hands, pretended to chase the men away. Only then was the bear's powerful tabu broken so that normal life could be resumed.

6

TRANSPORT, HOMES, EQUIPMENT AND CLOTHING.

Transport

The Lapps' methods of transport obviously differ greatly in winter and summer. In winter skis have been used by them for hundreds, even thousands, of years. Dozens of prehistoric skis have been found all over the North. They are broader and shorter than those known from the Middle Ages to modern times; 5–6½in (13–16cm) broad, 4–5½ft (1–2m) long. (Modern skis for beginners have reverted to comparable proportions). They are pointed at both ends, as are modern Lapp skis. From the Middle Ages until a century or so ago skis were of unequal length. A long ski (one as long as 12ft (4m) is known in Finland), hollowed underneath, was fastened on the left foot for running, a shorter one, often with sealskin on the bottom, on the right foot for pushing. A staff or the shaft of a spear or other implement served as a stick, with a wooden disc commonly attached as a basket. The skis had raised footholds and were often decorated with simple geometric designs. The Mountain Lapps used longer, narrower, skis than other groups. There is no record of the Lapps ever using snow-shoes.

Similarly, some form of sledge has been employed from the earliest times. The simplest, still occasionally used, is just a skin with the load placed on it and the edges drawn together to form a flat bag which is then pulled over the snow. Two types of sledge are found at present – the Lapps' special boat-sledge and the frame-sledge, in wide use in many

34 Crossing Russian Lapland (*Brooke, Bodleian Library*)

parts of the world. Bottom boards of what might have been an early type of boat-sledge and runners of small frame-sledges from as far back as the early Iron Age have been found in Finland and north Sweden. Sledges with runners, however, were reintroduced to Lapland only in the 1880s by Samoyeds moving into the Kola Peninsula. Drawn by two to four reindeer, they became the favourite passenger-sledge of the Skolts and have spread steadily elsewhere, being more capacious and easier to build than boat-sledges.

The boat-sledge, known by different names in different districts (*pulka*, *geres* and variants; *ackja* in Swedish) is distinctively Lapp (Illus. 35). It is thought to have evolved from a smaller hollow sledge used until quite recently by hunters in north Finland and Karelia. In its construction and in the names of several of its important parts it is similar to, or identical with, the smaller Lapp boats. There are three main types with local variations; the one-man driving *pulka*, the ordinary freight *pulka* and the 'lid' *pulka*, this being used to move the best food and most treasured possessions under the protection of a wooden cover with a lid. A typical driving/freight *pulka* from north Sweden is about 7ft (2m)

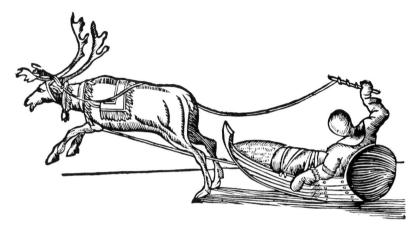

35 Reindeer-drawn sledge (*Scheffer, Bodleian Library*)

long, with a maximum width of 20in (50cm), 10in (25cm) freeboard and a back 17in (43cm) high. Corresponding figures for a covered model are 5½ft, 21in (1.6m, 53cm) 14in (36cm) to the top of the lid, and 16in (41cm). The forepart of the driving *pulka* used to be covered with seal-skin on a birchwood frame to protect the driver's legs. These sledges have

36 Driving and freight sledge, showing line of freight cover and detail of stern

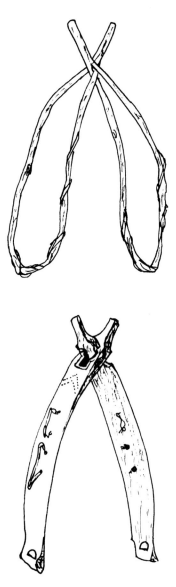

37 Pack-saddles. The top saddle is a temporary one made of two twigs joined together

a stout keel with vertical ribs to which four planks are fastened along each side to form the body. The back in particular is reinforced with iron straps. The normal load is about 220lb (100kg). The draught reindeer has for some time had a wooden collar attached to traces in place of the old harness, which consisted of a loop round the animal's neck just in front of its withers with a single trace going back between its legs. The rein now runs from a bit-less bridle and is held in the driver's hand. Previously it went back to, and was wrapped round, a driving-stick. The collar is usually gaily decorated and the animal has a bell on its neck.

In summer the Lapps move overland on foot carrying a pack or with pack-reindeer, on water by raft or boat. They never used wheeled transport until the advent of the motor age. A usual day's journey on foot is 25–30 miles (40–48km), nearly double under pressure. The 'legal load' has long been 38lb (17kg), but up to twice the amount is often carried in a skin rucksack. The Skolts use a bow-shaped container of Russian type. A stout staff is invariably used when walking, and the southern staff differs from the northern. The former is longer and originally had a metal point to be used in self-defence also, when covered with its broad, strong sheath, as a snow-shovel. The northern staff is about shoulder-height and its handle (which may also serve as a snow-shovel) is often of bone, beautifully decorated. Lapp staffs are thickest at the bottom which so balances them that they swing forward with the minimum of effort.

The simplest form of water transport, used in forest regions for crossing rivers or fishing in small lakes, is a raft of several logs, preferably of dried fir, kept together with cross-planks fore and aft, and propelled by a pole. But for many centuries the Lapps have made proper boats of several types. The large, sea-going, sewn-boats, for which they were once famous, have long disappeared. The sagas talk of two such made for a Norse chief, with twelve oars each side and 'not a nail was to be found in the boats. They were fastened together by sinews and osiers'. Smaller boats of this type were common into the eighteenth century. The Skolts made them with hemp rope until about eighty years ago.

Lapp boats have a pointed stern, except for a few short ones with a square stern, which gives the appearance of a larger boat cut in half.

Some may be; but there have been arguments about whether this shape and size, so similar to that of the *pulka*, might not represent an ancient, small, portable boat which influenced the development of the sledge. Forest and southern Lapps use a comparatively beamy boat, 16 to 20ft (5–6m) long. On the northern rivers longer, narrower boats, 24 to 28ft long, are preferred. The use of outboard motors has steadily increased since their introduction between the wars. Much formerly important, but seasonal, river traffic has been replaced by an extensive system of all-weather roads, which the Germans did much to develop when they occupied north Norway and Finland.

Homes

The classic Lapp home is the easily transported *kåhte* or *goatti* (a word related to 'cottage', but best known in the Scandinavian form, *kåta*) – a conical pole tent. Many peoples have constructions similar to the Lapps 'forked-pole' tent (*tjagge-kåhte*, *klykstångskåta*); the wigwam or tepee of

38 Bent-pole tent

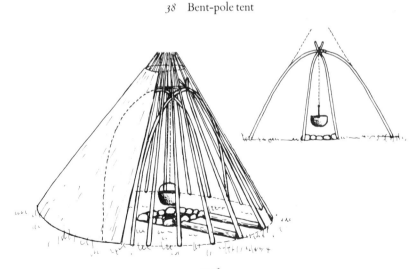

106

39 Lapp forked-pole tent in north Finland (*Studio B. Möller*)

the North American Indians is one example. But only the Lapps have the 'bent-pole' tent (*åtnåris-kåhte, bågstångskåta*), superior in several respects. For a long time now the mobile tent of the reindeer nomads has been of this latter type. Its appearance and method of construction may be seen in Illus. 38. It is of standard shape and size, oval, about 13ft (4m) from front door to the back, 15½ft (5m) across and about 11½ft (3.5m) high (10ft (3m) to the top of the wall). Because its main timbers, two pairs of curved poles from a birch tree of suitable shape, are shorter and lighter than the main poles (at least three) of the 'forked-pole' tent, as (by about 2ft (.6m)) are the side poles which support the fabric of the wall, it is easier to handle and transport. It is carried, together with the birch twigs for the floor, on the last sledge of the train. It takes about half an hour to erect or dismantle. Both types of tent have adjustable door-flaps and provision for a smoke-hole flap. Sheets of canvas are used for the tent walls in summer, a thicker cloth, originally hand-made, in winter; or, in olden days, skins. The 'forked-pole' type stands up better to high winds. The Lapps combine the advantages of both types by taking the more portable 'bent-pole' tent on migration and leaving frames of 'forked-pole' tents permanently at suitable staging sites to be covered with wall-fabric on arrival there.

Stronger permanent buildings were also constructed of baulks of timber to a similar basic conical design of mutually supporting members. The Skolt and Kola Lapps live, or until recently lived, in such homes with turf on walls and roof with birch-bark used beneath for insulation (*tarfe-kåhte, torvkåta,* 'turf hut'). The Forest Lapps put logs outside with stout planks inside (*påsse-kåhte, näverkåta* 'timber hut'). There are several different designs of both types. The Mountain Lapps have used both for winter quarters. Animals and stores are kept in smaller versions of such buildings, or in the former home when the family moves to an ordinary wooden house of common Scandinavian type; a process in train for well over a century and accelerated in Norway and Finland by the provision of subsidised new homes under

40 Old Lapp house and four-pole store (*aite*) near Ivalo, north Finland (*Arthur Spencer*)

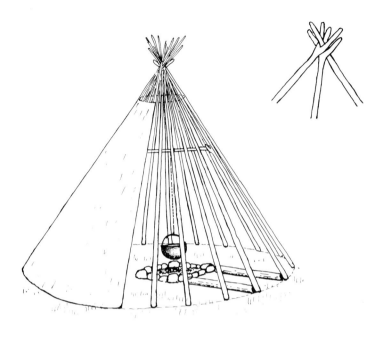

41 Forked-pole tent

the post-war reconstruction programme and in Sweden earlier by the general prosperity and increasing urbanisation.

Where people live in a confined space each part of their abode, on practical grounds, has its own functions. For the Lapps socio-religious considerations also influenced such a pattern. The old sacred area at the back of the tent has already been mentioned (p 88). It was marked off by a log on the floor. Logs are still used to delineate the entrance and hearth area, one on each side of the door reaching to the flat stones of the central fireplace. Behind this is a large flat stone for the kitchen area. The living space is on each side of these logs, the family on the left as one enters, others on the right. The floor is covered with reindeer skins above a thick layer of birch twigs. There are no chairs or tables, partly to avoid extra luggage, but mainly because one lies, or sits, on the floor, resting against a log, to keep below the smoke. The place of honour is near the hearth and it is very bad form to step between somebody and the fire. Northern Lapps often use individual canopies of thin material suspended from the roof to cover each sleeping place (usually for two persons for warmth) both for privacy and, in summer, to keep out mosquitoes. All sorts of belongings are also hung on the tent-poles to keep the floor uncluttered. On the ridge-poles, food is hung in the smoke for curing.

The stability of interlocking poles is utilised for many other constructions, large and small, from long fences for reindeer corrals to portable storage tripods. The various storage constructions, each with its specific function and name, are the most typical. The simplest (*påkkas*) is carried on migration and consists of three rods. Two rods have a hole near the top and when in use are joined by a dowel; the third, which rests in the fork thus formed, has a thong to wrap around the point of intersection and keep the device steady. It serves as a larder. Forked

42   Lapp tent and food store (*njalla*) (*Scheffer, Bodleian Library*)

43   *Aite* (pole-store). Note the fish drying (*Mauno Mannelin*)

sticks are assembled into tripods for many other uses where objects – a cooking-pot for example – have to be kept off the ground. Fishing nets are draped on long frames with forked tripod legs, *pulkas* rest on open platforms, provisions and various possessions on racks and platforms called *luovve*, some quite complicated, which are often covered against the weather. As Professor Ruong has demonstrated, these larger, covered constructions were almost certainly the origin of the pole-tent.

Pole-larders are another typical Lapp construction. These are small huts raised well above the ground on a pole, or poles. The *njalla* (Illus. 42) stands on a single stout pole about 6ft (2m) above ground to keep the meat stored in it out of reach of animals, particularly the wolverine, which may be further discouraged by downward-pointing spikes in the floor where it joins the pole, or by the pole being made slippery with grease. The owner enters it by means of a removable ladder, made from a tree-trunk with steps cut in it. This is the nomad's larder and, because of the Lapps' high standards of honesty, may safely be left unattended in the wilds. The *aite* (Illus. 43) has shorter legs at each corner, often formed from rooted trees cut off at a suitable height: sometimes one corner is supported by a growing tree. Similar store-huts are also put out of reach on the top of a smooth-sided rock. This type is used near, or in, encampments. There are several other versions, such as the *luopte* which is basically a longer *aite* but usually without sides, forming a strong, rectangular platform with a generously overhanging roof: an old fishing-net is hung over it to protect the contents from birds.

Equipment

Until quite recently the Lapps, like so many other peoples, had to make their equipment themselves from local materials – wood, bone, leather, roots. Metals came from outside their region and only small items such as blades for knives or tools, pewter-thread for embroidery and belt decorations were fashioned there. The emphasis was on small size, lightness and strength in the interests of portability. Both sexes carried essential implements on their person attached to a belt or in a pouch and still do. Their innate feeling for materials and lively sense of design produced objects both functional and beautiful – an aspect of Lapp life discussed in more detail in the next chapter. The tradition has been perpetuated for the commercial market and their own satisfaction by modern Lapp craftsmen.

Containers, of pinewood for heavy duty, otherwise of thin strips of birch-wood or (especially in Finland) birch-bark were – and to a lesser extent still are – made to carry goods and provisions on migration and the family's treasured possessions, including the baby in a birch-bark cradle lined with absorbent sphagnum moss. The bigger chests were reinforced with iron straps. Kegs and flasks for milk, salt or brandy, frames for storing cheeses near the top of the tent, the distinctive milking-scoops, cheese-moulds, were all made of wood, the smaller items being hollowed out from a single piece, preferably a knur of birch. Many

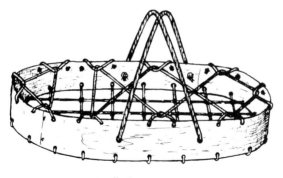

44 Cradle for pack-reindeer

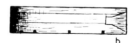

45 Cheese-mould: a) top; b) side; c) lid

other useful implements which would be of pottery or metal elsewhere were made of wood by the Lapps – for example pestles and mortars, hooks, dishes, cups, coffee-mills (the old type was a shallow wooden trough with a curved bottom along which a roller with a hand-hold each side of a central spindle was moved under pressure over the beans). Wood and metal were combined in many implements with handles – the knife which all Lapps carry, and a whole range of woodworking and special tools such as drills, saws, skin-scrapers and shammy-irons. Glues of reindeer hooves or fish, as mentioned earlier in the description of the laminated bow (p 73), were used to join, pine-tar to preserve, these wooden artefacts; and the use of sinew bindings and whippings was well developed. Pine roots boiled in lye were worked into a number of light, tough and almost waterproof, containers and dishes.

Bone was the other basic material. The toggle of the herdsman's lasso, spoons, the handles and sheaths of knives, hooks, shuttles and reeds for ribbon-weaving, needle-cases, staff-handles, frames for drawing pewter-thread; anything small, but ideally requiring more strength than wood provides, was of bone. It is also often preferred because it is better suited to the intricate decoration the Lapps delight in. Leather, ordinary and shammy, tanned in willow bark and sewn with leg sinews of the reindeer, was used for pouches, packs, belts and various items of clothing.

Clothing

The colourful traditional costume is still worn throughout Lapland on special occasions. Major items of it – dark jacket or skirt, cap, kerchief, belt and attachments, the excellent footwear – are the everyday wear of many, especially the older, Mountain Lapps in Finnmark and north Sweden. There are marked differences, especially in the caps, between various districts. A Lapp's dress thus proclaims his origin. The old wearing apparel, however, is much more than bright clothes of unusual styles. It was developed over a long period for special conditions. It combines excellent protection with freedom of movement and is very healthy. Originally it appears to have consisted almost entirely of furs in winter, with leather and, later, home-spun smocks in summer. The broadcloth tunic and skirt came in about a couple of centuries ago under the influence of contemporary Scandinavian fashions. Both have strips of cloth in the local colours down the sleeves, around the hem and on the revers. In this, as in other matters, the Skolts and eastern Lapps went their separate way. From the middle of the nineteenth century they have worn shirts, trousers and coats, and the women the long Russian skirt

46   Coiling sedge-grass to store for lining shoes (*Nordiska Museet, Stockholm*)

with shoulder-straps. The other Lapps, too, in the last few decades, have turned to ordinary ready-made clothes, since they are much cheaper and less trouble to acquire than the traditional costume with its intricate and time-consuming workmanship and now quite costly material.

Until a few years ago the standard winter wear for most Lapps was a reindeer-skin smock with the hair outside, reaching to the knee, or just below, and a belt. Beneath this another, shorter, smock was worn with the hair on the inside next to the wearer's body. This, like a string vest, provided good insulation. It also retained its warmth when wet. Lowland Lapps often wore woollen inner shirts instead and the women just a sheepskin coat with the fleece innermost. In severe weather a sort of poncho, of bear-skin for preference, oval with a central hole for the head, gave extra protection. This has now been replaced with a similar garment of stout cloth with a hood. Both men and women wear tight cloth trousers, over which leather breeches are drawn round the buttocks. These are attached to the tops of long leather leggings of reindeer leg-skin. Boots of the same skin cover the bottom of the leggings. Mittens, which keep the fingers warmer than gloves while leaving the thumb free to grasp rein or lasso, are also of this skin. In summer the long broadcloth tunic, occasionally a leather jacket, is worn over a skirt with tight cloth trousers and moccasins or boots of reindeer-skin or sealskin. Lapp footwear has no heels; this is better for walking than the modern fashion with a heel. Although woollen stockings are widely worn, boots and shoes, even with stockings, are filled with dried sedge-grass which is carefully combed and laid in a special way; it keeps the feet warm even when sodden and can easily be taken out and dried. The bottoms of the trousers or leggings are tied over the shoes by hand-woven ribbon bindings in the local colours.

The Lapps nearly always wear a belt, of cow leather among the Reindeer Lapps with metal or bone ornaments, of bright folk-weave for other groups. They like broad belts and are particular about wearing them in the correct position. For men, this is low on the hips, with the smock blousing out above it and the folds of the hem hanging regularly. The men have a sheath-knife attached to the left-hand side of their belts, the women a needle-case, scissors, sewing-ring (instead of a thimble) and similar odds and ends, and a knife by the right hip. A shammy pouch, usually in contrasting colours and often decorated with pewter-thread designs, hangs on a thong round the neck inside the tunic, or sometimes on the belt, with drinking-spoon, brandy cup, pipe, tobacco and so on. Beneath the neck-opening of the tunic a dicky of coloured cloth, embroidered with traditional tribal designs in pewter-thread, is worn in full dress.

47 Old Lapps sharing snuff. Note the skin trousers worn by the man on the right (*Nordiska Museet, Stockholm*)

Lapp caps are worth a special study in themselves. Men originally wore conical caps, of fur in winter, of wool in summer; women wore floppy caps with a high crown, usually tilted forward. These developed into more striking, colourful creations, with each district eventually having its own design and colour scheme. Early last century the men in many areas began to wear large caps with a high brim and four, long horizontal points – the 'four winds cap', based on a Russian fashion of the period. The Lutheran women turned to a cap with a high, rounded peak, curving forward like the Phrygian cornet of classical times. Both these were attacked by Laestadius and other fundamentalists as 'horned' or 'devil' caps. The women's fell into disuse about 1870, the men's are still worn in north Norway and Finland – with an otter-skin lining in winter.

Married Orthodox Skolt women have long worn a cap with a peak like a projecting tiara, decorated with red and white beads. Lapp women elsewhere replaced the 'horned' cap either with a smaller, round 'morning-cap' with ear-flaps, or with something like the earlier model, large with a floppy crown, tilted forward or backwards depending on the district. Each group's caps for single and married women and widows have different styles and colours.

Men's caps meanwhile diversified. Some acquired a leather peak, a practical eye-shade surprisingly lacking earlier, some a large, red pom-pom which enables the wearer to be seen far off. The Skolt men, however, have not worn typical Lapp headgear for decades, preferring knitted woollen helmets, large, flat Russian 'engine-driver' caps or, early this century, a felt hat like a trilby. These were supplemented in winter by a large cloth square underneath. Other Lapps, too, have increasingly turned to readily available outside styles for everyday wear – flat caps, ski-caps, fur-lined lumbermen's caps and the like.

7

LANGUAGE, LITERATURE, MUSIC AND ART

Language

Lappish belongs to the Fenno-Ugric group of the Ural-Altaic languages (Lappish, Finnish, Hungarian, Mordvinian, Cheremessian, Votiak, Syryen, Vogul and Ostiak). It is closest to Finnish and Hungarian, but shows the influence of several related tongues and has important affinities with the Uralic Samoyed language. It is thus out of the main stream of European languages and is extremely difficult to learn. The Lapps in fact speak three separate and mutually incomprehensible languages – south Lappish (spoken from the central Arjeplog district southwards), central, or north, Lappish (north from Arjeplog and as far east as Utsjoki) and eastern Lappish (from Inari eastwards). This is the usual division, but some authorities prefer to speak of seven main dialects – south, Ume, Pite, Lule, north, Inari (or Finnish) and Russian (also called Skolt and Kola) Lappish. There are many sub-dialects, from about twenty-five to fifty, depending on which expert is followed. Luckily north Lappish is understood by about three-quarters of all Lapps and since 1947 has been the standard written language in Norway and Sweden. A Nordic Lappish Language Committee was founded in 1971 to co-ordinate its development.

Both pronunciation and grammar are extremely complicated. There are, for example, 6 different vowel quantities, not just long and short. Vowel harmony and vowel assimilation are essential to proper speech,

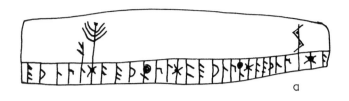

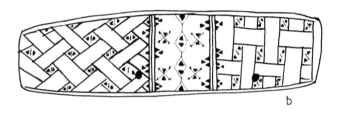

48 Old runic calendar: a) front; b) back

as are the correct gradation and accentuation of consonants: 'nn', for example, may be pronounced as two separate 'n's, or as a long 'n'. These subtleties are hard for outsiders to detect, much less to learn. Grammatically the outstanding feature is the cardinal importance of the verb. It has unfamiliar cases, such as essive (being in a state) and translative (changing from a state). It has 9 persons – 3 singular, 3 plural and 3 dual ('we two', 'you two', 'they two'). Nouns, too, have many cases, 6 in north Lappish, 8 in Lule Lappish. These make the use of prepositions largely unnecessary, since the concept is contained in the appropriately changed form of the noun. The locative case, for example, by indicating position does away with the need for a separate preposition such as 'at' or 'in'. There is a wealth of endings denoting diminutives. And different cases require a different pronunciation of the same syllables. There are no male or female genders, but a common and a neutral form.

The vocabulary is rich in words denoting concrete objects relevant to the Lapps' world, but poor in abstractions. Thus there are about 400 words dealing with reindeer and many denoting topographical features such as the condition of snow as it affects reindeer, travellers or hunters. Similarly there are many words for different degrees of kinship, which may laboriously be explained, but cannot be translated into languages of European origin.

The origins of Lappish are uncertain. It contains words which philologists claim to be able to trace back to archaic Uralic tongues of 6,000 years ago. There are other old survivals through Fenno-Ugric, Fenno-Permic, Fenno-Volgaic and Baltic Finnish. It is a philologist's paradise which, however, the ethnographers and historians invade, since such theories impinge on the study of the origins of the Lapps themselves. About 2,000 years ago loan-words began to enter the language from Finnish and Norwegian. These have often retained, or closely reflect, their contemporary form, now defunct in the original language. There is a close correlation between many Lappish and Finnish words. Many new words have subsequently evolved up to the self-evident modern *televisuvdna* or *radioaktivitetta*.

The first foreign glossary of Lappish, produced in 1557 by an English merchant on a voyage to Archangel, gives about a hundred words of Kola Lappish with Elizabethan-English equivalents. However, there are no Lappish grammars in English nor Lappish – English dictionaries, except in large works dealing with Fenno-Ugric word-lists. The monumental dictionary of Professors Konrad Nielsen and Asbjørn Nesheim gives the English, as well as the Norwegian, translation of the north Lappish words it lists. The ambitious young reader with philological ambitions has a virtually fresh field to plough!

Literature

The Lapps have a rich tradition of lyrical poetry and folk-tales, but it is only during this century that they have written them down in their own language. Very little has been translated into English. Two Lapp poems published by Scheffer in 1673, however, captured the attention of

German and Swedish poets and Longfellow and made a larger contribution to world literature than any Scandinavian works for many decades. They were given him by Olav Sirma, a Lapp student. Extracts translated by the author from a Swedish version are given below:

> Kulnasatj, my little reindeer,
> Time it is for us to go,
> Go we to the northern forests
> Hastening o'er the spreading marshes
> Journeying to the fair one's home.
> Hold me no longer, Kajgavare,
> Fare you well now, Kälvejaure . . .
>
> Shine warm, O sun, on Squirrel Water!
> Could I but climb up yonder fir-tree
> And know that I could see the Squirrel Water
> Where she is dwelling in the heather dale,
> Then would I fell each of the trees,
> The trees which now have grown too high;
> And all those branches would I lop
> Which now bear bright green leaves. . . .
> A boy's will is the wind's will,
> And the thoughts of youth are long, long, thoughts.
> If I should listen to them all,
> Then would I tread an evil path,
> One choice alone I must now make
> To find the way of truth.

The Lappish language was then already in use for religious publications. Lappish literature, however, really begins with the publication by Jacob Fellman in the 1820s of a couple of poems, although their authenticity has been questioned. More epics by a Lapp priest, Anders Fjellner, which appeared in 1876, caused a great sensation. Their genuineness, too, was disputed. It is now considered that both authors produced basically Lapp poetry, but embellished it with Finnish themes. Laestadius also at this period wrote tracts and recorded Lapp life in Lappish.

Lappish literature, however, first came into its own in the decade before World War I. Isak Saba, the first Lapp member of the Norwegian Parliament, was also a poet: his 'Ode to Lapland' (1906) has become the Lapps' National Anthem.

> Gukken dâvven Dawgai vuolde
> Sâbma suolgâi Sameædnâm:
> Duoddâr læbba duoddâr duokken,
> Jawŕe sæbba jawre lâkkâ,
> Čokkâk čilgiin čorok čæroin
> Allanâd'dik âlme vuos'tai,
> Šavvik jogâk, šuvvik vuowdek
> Cakkik cæggo stalle-njargâk
> Marâidæǵgje mærâidi . . .

> North beneath the Great Bear's stars
> Lapland looms, our silent land;
> Hills of purple, uplands gleaming,
> Lake on lake with shores aflood;
> Summits glisten; grey fells lowering
> Gauntly rise to Heaven's high vault;
> Rivers rush and forests sigh
> Dark cliffs pierce the foaming surf . . .

Matti Aikio, from Karasjok, next published several gloomy novels of Lapp life ; a Sea Lapp, Anders Larsen, a novel and a history of his people. In Finland, Pedar Jalvi from Utsjoki left a few fine poems and essays to mark his short life. But the greatest impact was made by Johan Turi, a Norwegian Mountain Lapp who spent his adult life in Sweden, with his vivid, masterly *An Account of the Lapps* (1910). This appeared with a Danish parallel text and is the only Lappish book available in an English translation. Lappish newspapers, at first short-lived, appeared in this period, the first in north Norway.

After World War I they settled down to more regular publication. Both through the personal influence of their editors, and the intellectual stimulus and platform they provided, they have subsequently played an important role in the development of Lappish literature. Torkel Tomasson, for example, first editor of the Swedish Lapps' *Samefolkets Egen Tidning* (The Lapp People's Own Paper) from 1919, was a distinguished amateur archaeologist. Among his regular contributors, Rector Gustav Park, also an author in his own right, made a major contribution to the growth of Lapp literary, and national, consciousness. Anta Pirak and Andreas Labba wrote of the Swedish Mountain Lapps, as did Nils Nilsson Skum who, like Turi, but with more art, illustrated his influential book *Same sita-lappbyn* (*The Lapp Village*) (1938), with brilliant drawings still in demand. Aslak Gutorm, from Utsjoki, with a novel and Paulus Utsi, another Swedish Mountain Lapp, with lyrical poems of great beauty, added to their people's heritage. These poems are in the old tradition and, with complicated and subtle rhythms and effective alliteration to which the language lends itself, depict the Lapp's passionate love of nature and the nomadic life:

> As long as we have water where fishes live,
> As long as we have land where wandering reindeer feed,
> As long as we have fells where wild things hide,
> Then have we solace on this earth.
> But when our home exists no more and our own land is desolate –
> Where can we then live?
> Our own dear land, staff of our life, has shrunk.
> The lakes have risen,
> The rivers are dry,
> The streams now sing a mournful song,
> The good land blackens, the green grass withers,
> The birds are quiet and flee . . .

(Paulus Utsi)

More recently a younger generation, benefiting from a more formal education and a more settled life, both conducive to study, has produced many works in prose and poetry. Lapps are also making their mark in the academic world, with Professor Ruong of Uppsala blazing the trail.

Many of these works spring from an old and rich oral tradition of poetry and folk-tales. The poetry is the distinctive sung lyric poem, which, since the words are subordinate to the song, is described in the discussion of Lapp music below. The folk-tales and myths are of three main types: the Stallo legends, the accounts of the Lapps' encounter with marauding bands of Chudes, and animal fables. There are very many of these stories: the Norwegian, Just Knud Ovigstad, published over 600 in the 1920s, and researchers still find new ones. Both Stallo and Chude legends undoubtedly enshrine, with many distortions and local embellishments, folk-memories of the Lapps' early encounters with powerful neighbours, Stallo being predominantly Norse, the Chudes Russo-Karelian. The Stallo stories are the more widespread and more complicated and more interesting to anthropologists and ethnographers. They are quite amoral with primitive, brutal themes and – a typical Lapp touch – many comic situations. The small, cunning Lapp invariably outwits the stupid, cruel giant and his wife and daughter. There are undertones of magic and of cannibalism absent in accounts of the Chudes. These people, too, are outwitted by the Lapps through their superior knowledge of the country, but are altogether more plausible. The Lapps, for example, lead them into traps and over precipices: many places all over Lapland (even where no Karelian ever set foot) are still known as 'Russian cliffs'. The colour of rocks of red stone, or covered with red lichen, is attributed to the Chudes' blood spilt on them.

The animal fables are less cruel and less grotesque, but again often reflect the Lapps' mischievous sense of fun. Bears, wolves, birds – particularly migrants with their mysterious habits – play a leading role, but the reindeer, perhaps because it is too familiar, scarcely features in them. The bear is usually quite friendly, but naughty: he will, for example, let girls he has caught go only when they lift up their skirts to show him they are not concealing a weapon there. Migratory birds are ruled by an old woman away in the south, to whose realm the large and the small travel together, the wagtail under the crane's wing, the cuckoo helping the dipper – until the dipper misbehaves. This is when she steals the cuckoo's jacket to keep warm, and is why the cuckoo so often chases the dipper calling *ko-ko-kop-to* (where is my jacket) which compels the dipper to fly into waterfalls. Dogs strike shrewd bargains with their owners; and many tales account for the appearance, or habits, of other animals.

Music

Traditional Lapp music is vocal, not instrumental. Its main feature is the rhythm and melody of the solo sung lyric poem, *juoigos,* 'yoik'. The words usually take second place to the music. Indeed, there need be no words: in the Jokkmokk and Arjeplog district especially, yoiking without words is a well-established tradition. Further north the text becomes more important and is often a poem in its own right. A *juoigos* is essentially the personal and spontaneous expression of any strong emotion. Anything may inspire it – a pretty girl, an attractive young man, a fine reindeer, a shimmering lake, a mighty mountain, thunder, a bear, a wolf, the welcome sight of one's tent, a spiritual experience. The actual text consists of a few words to announce the theme, which is repeated and developed in distinct periods rather than in separate verses of a set length. While searching for his next words the singer keeps going with a range of more or less standard sounds – *voia-voia, nana-nana, lu-lu-lu* and so on. Or he may improvise them in a way appropriate to his theme: thus a wolf-song is filled out with a howling *huoo-huoo-huoo.* Much depends on the performer's powers of recall. As Turi says, yoiking is 'the art of remembering other people'.

Each person aspires to his distinctive personal musical theme, his 'signature tune' known to all in his district. He can even get an acknowledged master of the art to produce one for him. Many themes are traditional favourites and have new words set to them, but it is bad form to use old words with new themes. Alliteration, onomatopoeia and the internal rhythms to which the language is particularly susceptible are used extensively. The following extracts from two yoiks are typical:

(Yoik from Jokkmokk)
I sing again from Ultevis,
I sing of Ultevis' high crags,
And the call of the reindeer hinds
And the tinkle of the leader's bell
Are heard together with my song.

126

Let them call, the hinds on Ultevis.
Let them rub their new horn's velvet
On the willow trees on Ultevis, on Ultevis . . .

(Yoik from Pite)

Oho! Oho! A song shall I sing,
Of these woods and Seuldetnjuoná,
The land between the rivers – aja! aja!
The woods where the waters flood over
Where one hears the call of calves
To their mothers, their mothers . . .
Never again shall I see them,
But my kin coming after
Will roam there . . . aja! aja! aaa . . .

Musically, the *juoigos* is deceptively simple. It sounds at first like a rather monotonous humming song, very difficult to describe. It is not like the yodelling of the Alps which is rather a merry bawling in an ordinary or falsetto voice. It is reminiscent of the muezzin call of Islam, but more complicated and more varied. Closer attention reveals a whole range of complicated cadences, changes of key, pitch and tempo. Full use is made of emotionally effective devices – *crescendo, diminuendo, glissando*, the *coup de glotte*, and other dramatic mannerisms – yet all within the limited range of the singer's voice and the conventions of the style. Some yoiks have a sinister, hypnotic, quality like an incantation. Indeed, they once were, and for this reason were banned by Christian missionaries. They cannot really be described nor, in fact, adequately represented solely by the musical notation of their themes. The words with their idiosyncratic intonation and accentuation and involved metrical form must be taken into consideration as an integral part of those yoiks which combine words with music. There are accordingly large, and growing, sound archives of the *juoigos* at Uppsala and Tromsø, and a few records and tapes are on public sale. There is some evidence that the Kola Lapps used also to hold epic song contests.

The old Lapp culture had only a few simple musical instruments. The drum has already been mentioned. There are also various rattles such as sticks with rings, boxes with stones inside; whistling devices such as a strip of bark or a feather between the lips; and, most interesting, a rudimentary form of oboe. This is made from a section, about 6 to 12in (15–30cm) long, of the stalk of an angelica plant, from which it gets its name, *fadno*. It produces a soft note like the middle range of a clarinet. The Lapps also use the instruments of their neighbours – the Finnish *kantele* (a form of psaltery), the concertina, the Swedish bark-trumpet – as well as, in recent times, more usual western instruments. Several Scandinavian composers have incorporated Lapp themes in their works; the Swede, Vilhelm Peterson-Berger, for example, in his symphonic rhapsody, 'Sameätnam'.

Art

Lapp art is basically artistic handiwork. The magic drums represent a rudimentary pictorial art, which may go back to Neolithic rock-paintings. With their suppression, however, and the aversion of the Lutheran, even more of the Laestadian, sect to pictures it was not developed further until this century. The eastern Lapps are again an exception. The artistic traditions of the Orthodox Church are reflected in their spirited secular pictures in the Russian folk style. They also decorate their buildings with painted or carved scenes from everyday life, especially of reindeer. Lapp sculpture otherwise – the ancient, crude, idols – hardly deserves the name. Their applied art is a very different matter. Light, precise, graceful and sometimes gay, it is a true reflection of their innate characteristics. In recent years it has been revived in almost every form. Lapp pride has provided the machinery, funds from central government and the drive of cultural and co-operative organisations such as *Sameätnam* the fuel. Traditional handicrafts are included in school syllabuses. Advanced courses of up to two years are available later. There is a whole new school of master craftsmen, who combine the best of traditional and modern styles and materials. Their success, it is true, has created a market into which much inferior stuff produced in factories further south has penetrated for sale to tourists. But their work nevertheless has brought the beauty of traditional Lapp art to

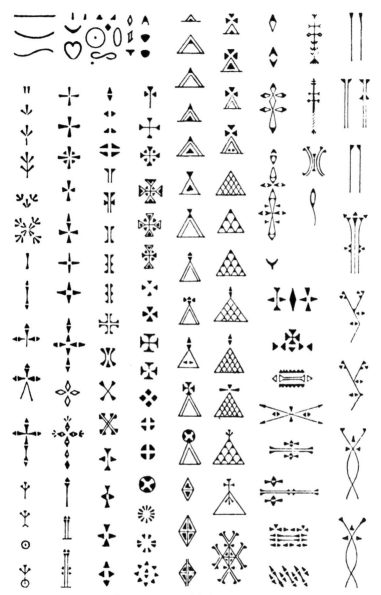

49   Southern Lapp motifs (*after Hampusson–Huldt*)

129

50   Sheath of horn decorated in southern style

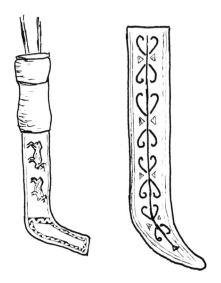

51   Knife-sheaths of horn decorated in northern style

the notice of the world. There has been a similar renaissance of old crafts among the Kola Lapps also.

The manufacture and adornment of horn implements is the most characteristic Lapp art form. It may also be the oldest. Designs still in use appear in cult-finds from the sixth century. Southern Lapp patterns reflect those of the Vikings. Lines, wedges and other figures – circles, ellipses, rhombs, in outline or solid – are the basic elements of design (Illus. 49). They are drawn with great delicacy and precision and in almost innumerable combinations. The pattern is picked out in soot-black. The southern style is abstract, geometrical and more sophisticated

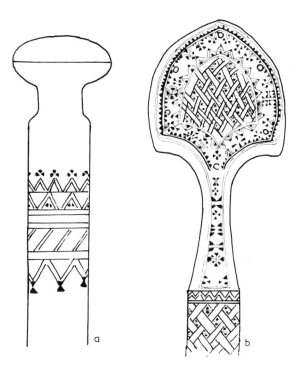

52 Bone handles for walking staffs: a) man's staff; b) woman's staff from Lyck-sele Lappmark (after Hampusson-Huldt)

than the heavier, and increasingly representational, style the north developed (Illus. 50 and 51). Interlaced patterns are favoured in the most southerly parts of Lapland, more open geometrical designs in the centre. Flowers and reindeer appear more and more in northern motifs. Master craftsmen – in Finland Nils-Aslak Valkepää, in Norway Per Hatta, in Sweden Lars Pirak, Esaias Poggats and Erik Tuolja to name a few – continue the old traditions and have widened the medium's use to modern items such as salt-cellars, linked belts and linked necklaces. They also use horn in new combinations with other old materials, in inlays, for example.

Pewter-thread embroidery was much used to decorate caps, collars, dickies, purses, spoon-pouches and reindeer harness until early this century. It was made by drawing a pewter wire by the teeth through holes in a gauge of horn, a smaller hole being used at each stage: thread as fine as 0.25mm has been made in this way. This metal thread is wound around another thin thread, formerly of sinew, recently of strong cotton, with the help of a distaff. The art, which had almost died out, was revived by Artur Jillker in north Sweden some years ago. His courses and demonstrations brought renewed popularity. Like other traditional Lapp crafts it has for some time been taught in schools. Similarly, suitable non-traditional uses have been found for it – on buttons, for instance, or modern jewellery – by the new generation of craftsmen.

The consciously artistic creations of experts, schooled in tradition and fully aware of the beauty and potentialities of their materials, have simi-

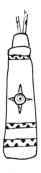

53   Needle-case of horn

larly replaced the simpler products of the old Lapp handicrafts. Milking-scoops, salt-flasks and such everyday objects are now produced for their intrinsic aesthetic appeal rather than as practical artefacts, which might incidentally also gratify the artistic senses. All Scandinavian peoples have a great feeling for wood and this is very apparent in modern Lapp handicrafts. The revival of the almost defunct skill of making containers from birch-roots is another illustration of the high quality of modern work, especially that of Ellen Kitok Andersson in Jokkmokk.

The traditional weaving of narrow strips of cloth on weaver's-reeds from homespun yarn was never as near extinction as some other crafts and has recently become widespread as a popular hobby. The natural

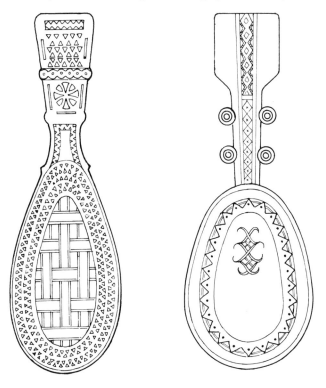

54 Horn spoon, southern style   55 Horn spoon, northern style

56 Silver jewellery (*Nordiska Museet, Stockholm*)

134

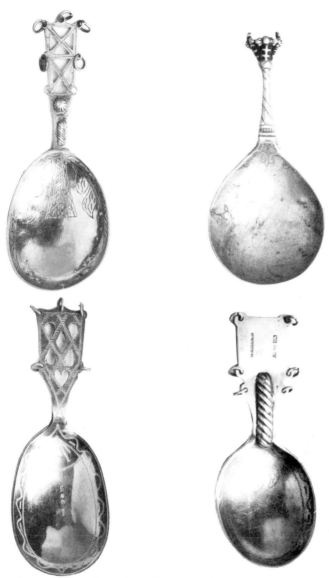

57 Good examples of traditional Lapp silver spoons (*Nordiska Museet, Stockholm*)

dyes such as alder-bark, crowberry or juniper twigs and other plants are used, the old colours and patterns of each district perpetuated in braid, belts and shoe-bindings; also, in recent years, in ties for tourists. New developments in textiles have also been made and several Lapp artists now produce tapestries and batik work.

The famous 'Lapp silver', of which examples may be seen in most Scandinavian museums, was never a Lapp art, except in so far as the Lapp customer had a large say in its design. Together with reindeer it represented the old Lapps' personal wealth. Hence the items are small – spoons with designs based on those of favourite horn spoons, necklaces, bracelets, rings. The men carried the spoon, often with a silver brandy cup, in a pouch, or hung them on chains round their necks. The Lapps themselves, however, did fashion small ornaments for belts or collars from thin silver plates and also moulded them. The new generation of Lapp craftsmen also includes silversmiths who produce much distinguished work in both traditional and modern styles. A favourite combination is a modern piece of jewellery which incorporates a traditional motif. These are often the more stylised symbols from the magic drums.

The first Lapp artist in the usual sense was Johan Turi, whose naïve illustrations to his book broke new ground. But the first artist of rank was the Norwegian Lapp, John Andreas Savio. Trained in Oslo and Paris and much influenced by Edvard Munch, he worked mainly in woodcuts. Although he produced many works in the contemporary European style his real appeal lies in his masterly depiction of his own Finnmark and its people. In Sweden, Nils Skum's drawings a little later provide a similar, but less expert, record. More recently Lars Pirak and Iver Jåks in Norway deploy a full range of techniques in oil and other media to portray Lapp, abstract and more general subjects.

8

THE LAPPS TODAY

One People in Four Countries

The emergence of a Lapp national consciousness, of a strong feeling of solidarity among all Lapps, is the most significant development among them today. The Kola Lapps in the USSR remain outside the mainstream of events, but in recent years their western kinsmen have shown more interest in their affairs both in their publications and discussions and by occasional, but increasingly frequent, visits. In the three Scandinavian countries the Lapps' reaction to the threat to their separate identity, which manifold external pressures pose, has become more coordinated and more political. Wider educational opportunities, mass media of information, social and economic developments, and the growing power of central government have all undermined the Lapps' special position. They are fast becoming just another group in a larger and more uniform society, many features of which are inimical to their cultural heritage.

In this changed situation the Lapps' old organisations – the Association of Finnish Lapps, the Norwegian Lapp Society, the National Federation of Swedish Lapps – have become more important. New ones have been founded; the most important of these is the Nordic Lapp Council, which was set up in 1956 by the three national organisations and has subsequently met regularly. Its aims are, on the one hand to promote in all Lapps a stronger and more constructive realisation of their role as Lapps in the modern world and, on the other, to defend their

rights and to guarantee their future as a separate people. Since 1972 it has had a permanent tripartite organisation, the Nordic Lapp Institute, at Kautokeino. This body inevitably has given a sharper edge to Lapp aspirations, political as well as cultural.

International trends too have played their part. The post-war era has been marked by the increasing attention paid to the rights, and the claims, of minorities. The United Nations Organisation has sub-committees to deliberate on, and holds conferences to discuss, these questions within the terms of its charter. New regional bodies, such as the Federal Union of European Nationalities, relay the message. All this is reflected in the Lapps' new attitudes, new organisations and new international contacts. Representatives of North American Indians, of the Kooroo and the Inuit People (formerly Australian Aborigines and Eskimos) now visit Lapland to discuss matters of mutual concern. Lapp spokesmen fly across the world to conferences on Arctic peoples and minorities.

Nor should strategic developments be overlooked as factors for change in the far north of Europe. The area's importance for the naval control of the North Atlantic was starkly illustrated by the German invasion of Norway in 1940. Subsequent shifts in the balance of power have enormously enhanced it. The ice-free waters of its coast provide the only unimpeded route for the Soviet navy to the Atlantic; most of Russia's nuclear submarines are based here. The rockets which form the forward land defences of Moscow and Leningrad are sited on the Kola Peninsula, along the Great Circle route from North America to western Russia. The NATO powers have a regional headquarters in north Norway. The neutral, well-armed, Swedes maintain important defence lines in Swedish Lapland, as the latest spy case at the end of 1976 has re-emphasised. Swedish iron ore from Kiruna, as events in World War II so clearly showed, is, in times of crisis, of great strategic, not merely econ-

58 Lakselv Church, Norway, which was built in 1970 to replace the old church destroyed in the war. At 72°N it is one of the most northerly churches in the world (*Arthur Spencer*)

omic, importance. The expansion of mining in north Norway and the growth of hydro-electric power generation are similarly of military significance, as will be the eventual exploitation of vast oil deposits in the Arctic Ocean.

The Impact of Post-war Changes

Events in Lapland since the war may conveniently be divided into three main phases. Firstly, reconstruction in the interests of survival; for a few groups, notably the Skolts, who chose to leave the Petsamo district when it became Russian and to settle in north Finland, this involved complete resettlement. Secondly, re-alignment to new and rapidly changing conditions, particularly in education and economic affairs and, thirdly, a reassessment of the situation thus created for Lapps as a minority more closely involved in a modern industrial society. It sometimes appears as if a fourth phase has now started, that of resistance to major recent trends, above all to what is widely held to be the undue encroachment of the State, especially in Sweden, on the Lapps' rights. Not all the countries concerned passed through all these stages; Sweden obviously had no war damage to repair. Nor did they go through them at the same time; Norway's desperate need caused her to take immediate steps which Finland, burdened with vast Russian war reparations, could not start on until much later.

The effects on Lapp life of the material aspects of post-war developments have been mentioned earlier – the changed pattern of life in permanent new houses of modern design, the switch to a cash economy, improvements in communications and the steady spread of machines and consumer goods. The whole ethos of the welfare state, interfering as well as assisting, has also had a profound psychological effect. A Skolt Lapp with an ex-serviceman's pension and other welfare payments living hundreds of miles from his old home in a modern house provided by the government clearly has a very different life from his former one. Far-reaching educational changes, too, have had major social, as well as intellectual, consequences. In Finland the children of minority groups have, from the inception of the republic, had a constitutional right to be taught in their mother tongue; in the three Scandinavian countries educational opportunities for Lapps are only now, after a series of reforms, broadly comparable in practice. But in Norway and Sweden the Lapps are not recognised in law as a separate minority for this, or other, purposes. In Finland and Sweden there are shortages of qualified teachers to instruct in Lappish.

Norway, where all schools and their contents had been destroyed by the 'scorched earth' tactics of the retreating Germans, was first to start post-war reforms. Here, as in Finland, there was a feeling that in the brave, new, world at peace and in gratitude for their wartime role the Lapps deserved better treatment. The high rate of illiteracy among Lapp

59   Lapps outside the church of Hetta in Enontekiö (*Matti Tirri*)

conscripts which an army report revealed spurred the work on. New schools were built, new text-books produced: one became a best-seller to curious tourists. Large sums were voted for Lapp education in the early 1950s. The high school at Karasjok was reopened, a vocational training centre set up at Kautokeino. The terms of reference of a commission appointed in 1956 to review the position of the Lapps included consideration of their educational opportunities on the basis that 'every child has a human right to receive its first instruction in its mother tongue'. The teacher training college at Tromsø had anticipated this by starting instruction in Lappish in 1954. From 1962 onwards the commission's recommendations were steadily put into effect. In 1969 parliament gave the Lapps the legal right to be taught in their own language. The Lapps in central Norway, too, have shared these recent improvements. At advanced levels the new University at Tromsø reserves a percentage of places for Lapps, teacher-training and medicine being important, and pursues Lapp studies to degree standard, as Oslo University has done for many years.

In Sweden, since the abolition of the nomad-schools in 1955, Lapp children have been educated either at local primary schools or in special sections of other schools – an expensive system costing about five times the national average. Senior pupils attend high schools, notably the famous Lapp Folk High School in Jokkmokk. Numerous short courses, many residential, are held for young and old in Lapp language and culture, those on handicrafts being very popular. At the end of 1976 courses were started even in the very difficult Southern Lapp language. Uppsala University has long included Lapp studies in its curriculum and the new university at Umeå now provides further opportunities. More Lapps are going on to other branches of higher education also.

In Finland basic schooling, where there are suitably qualified teachers, is given to Lapp children in their own language. But the difficulties of the language itself have impeded progress to this goal. For example, at a school opened in 1972 at Sevettijärvi to teach children in their own dialect only a limited impact was made because it was spoken in such a small area. Nevertheless, the commission investigating this reiterated the basic principle that, in spite of difficulties, the aim should still be to teach children in their own language. Meanwhile they are taught in Finnish as they are in all high schools except the Lapp Christian High School at Inari. Helsinki University has a well-established tradition of Lapp studies. Turku University runs its Sub-Arctic Research Institute at Kevo, near Utsjoki, the most northerly permanent such station in the world. The new University of Uleåborg has had Lapp studies on its curriculum since its foundation in 1970, with a professor in charge since 1973.

It is difficult to disentangle the role played by Lapp organisations in the various post-war changes. Much of what has happened would, in broad terms, have happened anyhow; but there is no doubt that the opinions expressed with increasing frequency and volume by the Lapps have influenced the pattern of events. In particular the national governments have in the last few decades paid much closer attention to their situation. The latest manifestation of this is the compendious report on Lapp affairs completed after four years' deliberations by a Swedish commission at the end of 1975. Also in Sweden, during the electoral campaign in the autumn of 1976, a cabinet minister made a special appeal for Lapp support by promising them a much bigger say in their own affairs in future. To that extent the Lapps have now become a political force. But they have influence rather than power. Through programmes on television and radio these last ten years, backed by opinion polls and supported by articulate, progressive opinion among their fellow-countrymen, the Lapps' present situation has become well-known to the general public. It is now a permanent factor in the political equation.

A Lapp nationalist movement is thus now established and well publicised. But to talk of Lapp nationalist political parties is unrealistic. A Lapp National Day, as proposed at the end of 1976, may come in time to be celebrated on 8 November on the anniversary, of all things, of the murderous riots in Kautokeino in 1852. But the Lapps are too few and too widely dispersed over three countries in many electoral districts, including Stockholm, Oslo and other big cities, to form an effective power base. And the pattern of their voting has so far reflected that of the electorate at large, with the older generation tending towards conservative views.

Somewhat ironically in view of her enlightened traditions, it is in

143

Sweden that Lapp reactions to present trends are most marked. The force of circumstances drives both sides. With the highest standard of living in the world and the second largest consumption of energy per head, Sweden must exploit all her resources to the full for the benefit of all her people. These include the riches of Swedish Lapland. Their development inevitably and increasingly harms the Lapps. Under pressure they react more strongly and come into conflict with the State. The decision of the High Court in September 1976, in the long drawn-out 'Skattefjäll Case' in which the Lapps were appealing against certain developments proposed on their reindeer lands by State enterprises, is the latest illustration of this. To the Lapps the judgement, confirming the State's powers to act in this way, is a 'judicial scandal'. To the State, which has owned these areas for centuries (p 40), it is the assertion of a right it has not previously chosen to exercise. The State's decision to build dams for power stations in areas designated as National Parks and therefore legally inviolate is another ground for complaint. There is room for plenty of conflict in this ambivalent situation where the State is both party to and judge of such disputes, at a time when the country's well-being requires the fullest possible use of its resources.

In Finland and Norway the problem is less acute. Their populations are smaller, their needs more limited. The topography and resources of their Lapp territories differ from Swedish Lapland. Norway has vast reserves of energy and her northern minerals are worked on the coast well away from the Lapps' homeland. But the underlying problems are the same. The basic dilemma of a minority in a plural society remains. To what extent can the Lapps adapt themselves to modern developments without losing their national heritage in the process?

Integration Versus Identity

The position of the Lapps today provides a striking illustration of the problems of a small culture in ever closer contact with a larger. As individuals their response varies from integration into the dominant society to virtual repudiation. Many Lapps, both in their own areas and the big cities further south, are full members of the community at large with occupations lacking any specifically Lapp connotation – a Norwegian cabinet minister, a Swedish provincial governor, officials, members of parliament and less exalted jobs for example. Their numbers grow as a better educated younger generation seeks to match its aspirations. In doing so, however, they break with and, it could be argued, weaken, their people's heritage. They also tend to seek work outside Lapland. So do some of their less well endowed fellows, whose lot is what may be called negative integration, or structural discrimination.

60   Reluctant passengers at Rovaniemi, north Finland (*SML*)

61 (previous page) Interior of a home in Ollila, Utsjoki. Notice that there is no electric light (*Hiroyasu Kurashina, Japan*)

This second category comprises the victims of economic and social changes in the North. Their old livelihood has gone. The new enterprises demand a higher level of skill and more expert knowledge than they possess. The great iron mines at Kiruna are a prime example of this. A marvel of modern technology and the nucleus of a thriving town, they provide few, and only the most menial, jobs for Lapps, in whose old lands they operate. The same applies to other major projects such as hydro-electric developments, the power from which in any case goes largely to southern industry. Hence there has in recent years been a serious demographic imbalance among the Lapps, as many women of marriageable age seek work outside Lapland and aging bachelors remain alone to live out their more traditional lives. Among many Lapps, particularly those with memories or dreams of the old ways, there has grown feelings of hopelessness, alienation and bewilderment.

Active discrimination, quite common in Norway until recently, has largely disappeared. This once caused many Lapps to do their best to conceal their different origins and qualities in self-defence. 'Speak Lappish below decks, Norwegian above', was the advice of Lapp fishermen to their sons when putting into a Norwegian port. Similarly, the Norwegian census of 1950, which classified Lappish-speakers separately, was notoriously inaccurate because, for the above reasons, the inhabitants of districts in Finnmark which had had large Lapp populations for centuries did not want the fact that they spoke Lappish to be recorded. All this has changed. But the unwitting structural discrimination, which circumstances impose on the less well equipped Lapps in a labour market which increasingly requires qualities they do not possess, is probably an even greater handicap. Its effect on the Skolt Lapps has been mentioned earlier (p 61).

In these circumstances the aim of the more politically active Lapps today is to reach a satisfactory synthesis of old and new, to identify the essential features and lasting values of their heritage and, as far as possible, retain and strengthen them within a larger society modified to ensure their survival. They expect the same status, and opportunities for the same standard of living, as their fellow citizens. To quote the words of the Norwegian professor, Harald Eidheim, a forceful protagonist of Lapp rights from the 1950s, in *Men and Milieu in North Norway* (Oslo, 1971), one of the first steps towards this could be the acquisition of 'an official ethnic status in addition to their citizenship'. The assumption is that, as a recognised minority, they would have a stronger claim to special treatment. However, the basic concept of the universality of a modern democracy raises obstacles here. Moreover, although another Lapp champion, Professor Edmund Dahlström of Gothenburg, in *The Lapps – one People in four Lands* (Stockholm, 1974), has correctly stated that 'the unspoken condition of action by certain authorities is that Lapp life should disappear with poverty in North Sweden', such a criticism, although accurate, is not the whole truth. Nor does it comprehend all the issues of practical politics involved: the authorities thus criticised have the wider interests of the whole community to serve.

Such analyses have greatly helped to publicise the situation of the Lapps: and their own spokesmen now make the running. To what extent the Lapps' particular interests as they see them can be reconciled with the demands of the countries of which they are part remains to be seen. At a period of economic stress like the present they are likely, as the Skattefjäll case shows, to be subordinated to them. In the long run the best solution appears to be to treat them as a minority, with or without formal juridical status as such, and to concentrate on diverting to their use more of the wealth created by the exploitation of their territory. This could be spent both as larger subventions to support traditional activities at the heart of their culture, primarily reindeer-breeding, and on the promotion of light industry, particularly traditional handicrafts. There are, after all, very few Lapps in the world. They live mainly in countries which are rich by world standards and have responsive and enlightened governments. The cost in monetary terms would be slight. But the cost to the cultural and spiritual heritage of the world of the gradual extinction of this unique and attractive people would be enormous. Let us hope that, as the Lapps' situation becomes better known and their case more widely acknowledged, it will never have to be paid.

SELECT BIBLIOGRAPHY

As well as indicating this book's main sources in English, the Bibliography is designed to give a lead to those wishing to go further into particular aspects of Lapp life and culture. Most of the works listed themselves have a bibliography which will facilitate this. The publications of learned societies – the *Journal of the Royal Anthropological Institute* and *Man* in this country, the *Anthropological Quarterly* in the United States, for example – open up other lines of research. The ethnographic departments of universities and museums are a further source of such information, as are the occasional symposia produced by his colleagues to honour a noted Lappologist. Only *Lapponica* in honour of Professor Israel Ruong is mentioned below, but there are several others of great value.

No attempt has been made to list the occasional short articles of very varying quality in general publications such as *The Geographical Magazine* or *The Times Educational Supplement* in England, *The Journal of the National Geographic Society* in America, or on the feature pages of numerous magazines and newspapers. Some books available have been omitted as making little contribution to the subject beyond a personal account. Equally, standard works on special subjects such as flora, fauna, geology or climate, which only incidentally deal with Lapland, are not included.

Sooner or later, however, any serious student of the subject will require a working knowledge of at least Norwegian and Swedish to keep up to date. There is, for example, practically nothing published in English on the important changes in the Lapps' political attitudes in the last decade. These are best reflected in their own regular publications such as the Swedish Lapps' monthly publication, *Samefolket*. Other topics are continuously up-dated in the publications of Scandinavian learned societies and museums. Finally, it is the author's hope that his book will encourage some younger readers to learn Lappish in order to make a deeper study of this remarkable small people than his own age and circumstances now permit.

The following are the most important works on the Lapps in English:

Acerbi, Joseph. *Travels through Sweden, Finland and Lapland to the North Cape* (London, 1802)

Alfred the Great, King. *The Compendious History of the World by Orosius*, English translation by J. Bosworth (London, 1855)

Allison, Anthony, C. and others. 'The Blood Groups of the Swedish Lapps', *Journal of the Royal Anthropological Institute*, 86 (1956)

Beckmann, Lars. 'On the Anthropology of the Swedish Lapps', in *Lapponica* (qv)

Bergsland, Knut. 'Norwegian Research on the Language and Folklore of the Lapps, Part I, Language', *Journal of the Royal Anthropological Institute*, LXXX (1950)

Bonaparte, Prince Roland. *A Note on the Lapps of Finnmark* (Paris, 1886)

Brooke, Sir Arthur de Capell. *Travels through Sweden, Norway and Finnmark to the North Cape* (London, 1823)

—— *A Winter in Lapland* (London, 1827)

Butler, Frank Hedges. *Through Lapland with Skis and Reindeer* (London, 1917)

Clarke, Edward Daniel. *Travels in various countries of Europe, Asia and Africa*, Part 3: Scandinavia, Vols 9–10 (London, 1824)

Collinder, Björn. *The Lapps* (Princeton, London, 1949)

Consett, Matthew. *A Tour through Sweden, Swedish-Lapland, Finland and Denmark* (London (Stockton), 1789)

Christiansen, Reidar Th. 'Norwegian Research on the Language and Folklore of the Lapps, Part II: Mythology and Folklore', *Journal of the Royal Anthropological Institute*, LXXX (1950)

Cramér, Tomas. 'Rights of the Same to Land and Water', in *Lapponica* (qv)

Crottet, Robert. *Lapland* (London, 1968)

——. *The Enchanted Forest*, with commentary by Eric Linklater (London, 1949)

De La Motray, Aubry. *Travels through Europe, Asia and into Part of Africa* (London, 1724)

Elbo, J. 'Lapp Reindeer Movements across the Frontiers of Northern Scandinavia', Scott Polar Research Institute, *Polar Record*, Vol 6, No 43 (Cambridge, 1952)

Emsheimer, Ernst, 'A Lapp Musical Instrument', *Studia Ethnomusicologica Eurasiatica* (Stockholm, 1964)

Fjellström, Phebe. *Lapskt Silver*, with English Summary: *Lapp Silver* (Stockholm, 1962)

——. '*Archangelica archangelica* in the Diet of the Lapps and the Nordic Peoples', in *Lapponica* (qv)

Gjessing, Gutorm. 'The Norwegian Contribution to Lapp Ethnology', *Journal of the Royal Anthropological Institute*, LXXVII (1947)

——. *Changing Lapps*. Monographs on Social Anthropology No 13, London School of Economics and Political Science (1954)

Graff, Ragnvald. 'Music of Norwegian Lapland', *Journal of International Folk Music Council*, VI (1954)

——. 'Knots used by the Lapps', in *Lapponica* (qv)

Hakluyt, Richard. *The Principle Navigations, Voiages, Traffiques and Discoveries of the English Nation* (London, 1598–1600; Ed John Masefield, London and New York, 1906)

Hill, Rowland G. P. (Ed). 'The Lapps To-day in Finland, Norway and Sweden', *Conference of Jokkmokk, 1953, and Karasjok, 1956*, Le départment de Lapponie, Paris (1960)

Hulkekrantz, Åke. 'Swedish Research on the Religion and Folklore of the Lapps', *Journal of the Royal Anthropological Institute*, LXXXV (1955)

Hyne, C. J. Cutliffe. *Through Arctic Lapland* (London, 1898)

Itkonen, Toivo I. 'The Lapps of Finland', *Southwestern Journal of Anthropology* (Albuquerque, 1951)

Karsten, Rafael. *The Religion of the Samek* (Leiden, 1955)

Lapponica. Essays presented to Israel Ruong, Studia Ethnographica Upsaliensia XXI (Lund, 1964)

Leem, Knud. 'An account of the Laplanders of Finnmark', in Pinkerton's *General Collection of Voyages and Travels in all Parts of the World*, Vol I (London, 1808)

Linnaeus, Carl. *Iter Lapponicum 1732*, Translated into English by J. Edward Smith as *Lachesis Lapponica, A Tour Through Lapland* (London, 1811)

Lowie, Robert H. 'A Note on Lapp Cultural History', *Southwestern Journal of Anthropology* (Albuquerque, 1945)

Magnus, Olaus. *Carta Marina* (Venice, 1539) with English commentary by Edward Lynam (London, 1949)

——. *Historia de Gentibus Septrentionalibus* (Rome, 1555)

Manker, Ernst. 'Die lappishe Zaubertrommel', *Acta Lapponica,* I and VI (Stockholm, 1938 and 1950)

——. 'The Swedish Contribution to Lapp Ethnography', *Journal of the Royal*

Anthropological Institute, LXXXII (1953)

——. 'The Nomadism of the Swedish Mountain Lapps in 1945', *Acta Lapponica*, VII (Stockholm, 1953)

——. 'Lapparnas Heliga Ställen', with English summary: 'The Lapps' Sacred Sites', *Acta Lapponica*, XIII (Uppsala, 1957)

——. 'Fångstgropar och Stalotomter', with English summary: 'Trapping Pits and "Stalo-sites"', *Acta Lapponica*, XV (Uppsala, 1960)

——. *People of Eight Seasons* (Gothenburg, 1963; London, 1965)

——. 'The Bone Age of the Lapps', in *Lapponica* (qv)

——. 'Skogslapparna i Sverige', with English summary: 'The Forest Lapps in Sweden', *Acta Lapponica*, XVIII (Stockholm, 1968)

Manker, Ernst and Vorren, Ørnulv. *Lapp Life and Customs* (London, New York, Toronto, 1962)

Marsden, Walter (Ed). *Lapland,* in Time – Life series on the World's Wild Places (Amsterdam, 1976)

Nesheim, Asbjørn. *Traits from Life in a Sea Lapp District* (Oslo, 1949)

——. 'The Lapp Fur and Skin Terminology and its Historical Background', in *Lapponica* (qv)

——. *Introducing the Lapps* (Oslo, 1971)

Nickul, Karl. 'The Skolt Lapp Community in Suenjelsijd during the Year 1938', *Acta Lapponica*, V (Stockholm, 1948)

——. 'Place Names in Suenjel – a Mirror of Skolt History', in *Lapponica* (qv)

Paine, Robert. *Coast Lapp Society,* Vols I–II (Tromsø, 1957 and 1961)

——. 'Lapp Betrothal', in *Lapponica* (qv)

——. 'Animals as Capital', *Anthropological Quarterly*, Vol 44, No 3 (Washington DC, 1971)

——. 'The Herd Management of Lapp Reindeer Pastoralists', in *Perspectives on Nomadism*, International Studies in Sociology and Social Anthropology (Leiden, 1972)

Pehrson, Robert H. *The Bilateral Network of Social Relations in Könkämä Lapp District* (Oslo, 1964)

Pelto, Pertti J. *Individualism in Skolt Lapp Society* (Helsinki, 1962)

——. *The Snowmobile Revolution: Social Change in the Arctic* (University of Minnesota, 1973)

Porsanger, Samuli. 'The Sense of Solidarity among the Lapps', in *Lapponica*

Ruong, Israel. *The Lapps in Sweden* (Stockholm, 1967)

Rönn, Gunnar. *The Land of the Lapps* (Stockholm, 1961)

Scheffer, Johannes. *Lapponia* (Frankfurt, 1673), translated into English as *The*

History of Lapland (Oxford, 1674)

Simonsen, Povl. 'The History of Settlement', in *Norway North of 65* (London, 1960)

Sutherland, Halliday. *Lapland Journey* (London, 1938)

Tirén, Karl. 'Die lappische Volkmusik', *Acta Lapponica*, III (Stockholm, 1942)

Turi, Johan Olafsson. *Turi's Book of Lapland*, translated from Danish by E. Gee Nash (London, New York, 1931)

Utsi, Mikel. 'The Reindeer-Breeding Methods of the Northern Lapps', in *Man*, Vol IV (London, 1948)

Vorren, Ørnulv. 'Lapp Settlement and Population' in *Norway North of 65* (London, 1960)

———. 'The Reindeer Industry', in *Norway North of 65* (London, 1960)

———. 'The Modern Lapps', *Paper to Circumpolar Symposium*, Alaska (1967)

———. 'Some Trends of the Transition from Hunting to Nomadic Economy in Finnmark', in *Circumpolar Problems* (Pergamon Press, Oxford, New York, 1972)

Vorren Ørnulv and Manker, Ernst. *Lapp Life and Customs* (London, New York, Toronto, 1962)

Whitaker, Ian. 'Social Relations in a Nomadic Lapp Community', *Samiske Samlinger* 2 (Oslo, 1955)

Wickman, Bo. 'The Swedish Contribution to Lapp Linguistics', *Journal of the Royal Anthropological Institute*, 89 (1959)

INDEX

(Numerals in italics denote illustrations)